Praise for THE POWER OF WHY NOT

"Raising confident children who can excel at school and in life is the goal of all parents and teachers. Namita's practical program for possessing A Confident Mindset™ has helped our students and their parents navigate the challenges of today's world. *The Power of Why Not* is an indispensable guide for parents, teachers and children."

Lisa Luther, Principal, Brookfield Elementary School, Troy, MI

"I participated in the ConfidentLee® program in elementary school. I wasn't sure what to expect, but it turned out to be a game changer. It has helped me give opportunities a shot both in middle school and in high school. I take the 'why not' approach in life because I know what it takes to become confident."

Sanjana Kesireddy, Detroit Country Day School, Beverly Hills, MI

"Our entire school community from toddler through middle school adopted A Confident Mindset™ program following an intensive professional development for the entire staff. The curriculum is age/grade-specific and encourages open discussion as well as private reflection. The result is astounding! Staff and students are more open to attempt new skills, explore freely, and support one another as champions and rocks. This guidebook should be on the nightstand of every parent and the curriculum should be implemented in every school."

Jennifer Brown, Head of School, Birch Grove University Prep, Oakland Charter Township, MI

"My children participated in the confidence building program and benefitted greatly. I want to support them at home as well. This practical guide offers a step-by-step process for me to do so. I love the fact that my children find the activities fun and engaging. Our whole family now has a unified understanding of what confidence means. The children now know that do not need to 'be confident' at the get go but will 'become confident' after actions of practice. This has opened their mind to giving things a shot and instilled in them the 'why not' approach. All parents should add this book to their collection."

Renukha Subash, Parent of Adhi (age 11) and Iniya (age 8), Sterling Heights, MI

THE POWER
OF WHY NOT

THE POWER OF WHY NOT

A Guide to Raising Confident Children Who Are Happy, Kind and Successful

NAMITA PRASAD

Published by ChildsFeet Press

Contact information: www.namitaprasad.com

ISBN (paperback): 979-8-9853249-0-7
ISBN (ebook): 979-8-9853249-1-4

Cover Design: Eric Labacz
Interior Design: Christy Day
Editor: Debra Englander

Printed in the United States of America

Dedication

To Pops, my first champion,
You believed I did not need to be rescued because
you had taught me to "become confident."

To Mom, my rock,
You are my biggest critic and cheerleader.

To Karishma and Rohan,
my older two kids,
I am proud that you are carrying on Pops' mantra.

To Maahi,
my youngest child, If it wasn't for you,
I may not have found my calling.

CONTENTS

INTRODUCTION

WHY I WROTE THIS BOOK

"**W**hy do I need to try this? I don't think I can do this. I won't be any good at it." You have probably heard a child say these sentences all too often. I know I said it as a child and have heard it frequently as a parent and educator. Adults have good intentions. They want to do the best that they can with the resources they have. When they offer a child an opportunity, all they want is for the child to give things a shot by choosing "why not" over "why." My own life journey and work with children made me realize that the bridge from why to why not requires having confidence.

+ What is confidence?
+ Can anyone become confident?
+ Does the confidence of the adult reading this book affect their role in developing confidence in a child?

The answers to these questions are the subject of this book. Instilling confidence in a child doesn't happen overnight. It is a step-by-step process. A child must first understand what confidence is before he or she can build it. Equipped with this foundational knowledge, the child is empowered to explore opportunities.

Building confidence allows the child to have the power to say "why not" instead of defaulting to "why," even when unsure of himself. The "why not" approach to life opens the doors to personal growth. Thus, it's imperative we help the child develop confidence from an early age.

If having confidence is so pivotal in a child's life, why are most children not taught systematically how to become confident?

I believe there are some misconceptions we have about confidence that, if not debunked, can hold us back from making progress:

- **Misconception 1:** What confidence means to me is the same as it means to you. This is not always the case. Confidence is interpreted differently from person to person. When people use varying definitions for the meaning of confidence, it can create confusion for children.
- **Misconception 2:** Confidence is a skill and can be taught like other skills the child is learning. Some adults believe that confidence is a skill like music, swimming, or art. Confidence is not a skill. Confidence is what defines a child's approach not just to music, swimming, art but to life itself.
- **Misconception 3:** If children can speak in front of a group of people, they are confident. Being able to deliver a speech or communicating with others is important; however, it is not the same as being confident.
- **Misconception 4:** Adults need to be confident before they can help a child develop confidence. Adults often believe, mistakenly, they must be a confident person; otherwise, they can't be an effective confidence builder.

Children unknowingly feel the pressure to be confident from the get-go and adults feel the pressure to first be confident themselves before they can develop confidence in a child. This pressure is deeply rooted in these misconceptions. To debunk these misconceptions, I started teaching confidence building programs and ultimately founded ConfidentLee® (a confidence building program).

Since 2014, I've been on a mission to instill confidence in children by serving families through my academic centers and confidence building programs in Michigan. I have interacted with scores of adults who have shared a common desire to see their children become confident. This led me to devise curriculum that would explain what confidence is, why it should be developed, and how to instill it in a child. I have connected with many educators who have shared stories about their eagerness for confidence development in schools.

I have been teaching confidence building since 2015. Witnessing the outcome has made it clear that children became empowered when they developed a mindset of confidence. This mindset led them to embrace the power of "why not." The outcome of possessing such a mindset was positive. A coach told me a child who had taken our program was willing to try robotics, even though he wasn't sure he would be good at it. A parent happily shared with me that her child became more helpful at home and viewed doing dishes daily as his contribution to the family, rather than a chore. A teacher was excited that a student who had taken our course worked harder on his homework without worrying too much about the outcome of the upcoming test. I have seen firsthand how instilling confidence in children has provided benefits not only in the classroom but in life.

The curriculum includes robust and engaging activities to teach the confidence building process. The best compliment I received was a parent telling me, "My child wasn't too happy about being enrolled in your confidence building program; but after the first class, he couldn't wait to come back." With the impact and outcomes ConfidentLee® has made in such a short time, adults often ask about the strategies they can use to build confidence in children.

I hope to build confidence in children around the world just as we are doing in our local region. However, I know our process for building confidence needs to be taught beyond our classrooms. Children need confidence today and they should not have to wait.

For this reason, I have created confidence building curriculum and I've written this guide, *The Power of Why Not*, to help adults who want to instill confidence in a child. I refer to the term "well-meaning adult" throughout this book. I am referring to you, the reader. You have chosen to have a positive influence on a child's life. I present this book to you as both a partner and resource. This book is filled with real-world, practical experiences to demystify what confidence is as well as provide a step-by-step process on how to build it.

You might be saying: My plate's already full with their academics, sports, and extracurricular activities! Now I need to teach my children how to become confident? Really?

Developing confidence in a child may seem like an overwhelming task, especially when there are so many skills and attributes adults already impart to children in their formative years. The goal is not to add to your full plate, but rather to lighten the load.

You may ask yourself; Can I develop confidence in a child? No child is born confident, and an adult's own confidence level should not prevent him or her from being able to develop confidence in a child. Some of us were offered the gift of being raised by parents to become confident, and others were not. I was fortunate to have confidence instilled in me from a young age. This helped pave the life I have made for myself despite all my trials and tribulations as a single mother and entrepreneur.

Understanding the impact that confidence has had on the trajectory of my life, I became determined to share with others what I learned: **Confidence building needs to be intentional, not circumstantial, and it needs to start in childhood.**

I wrote *The Power of Why Not* to share everything I've learned as a confidence educator, entrepreneur, and parent. Whether you—the well-meaning adult—is a parent, grandparent, coach, educator, or caregiver, the steps for instilling confidence, outlined in this book, will be transformational.

ABOUT THE POWER OF WHY NOT

The *Power of Why Not* is grounded in practicality—that of a mother and an educator. I've filled the chapters with my own life experiences, the techniques we use at ConfidentLee®, tools and resources to use with your child, and real stories from our classrooms. In most cases, the names and personal information have been changed to preserve privacy. Several exchanges have been recreated from memory, and I have presented them to the best of my ability.

The Power of Why Not provides a resource for all well-meaning adults who want to instill unstoppable confidence in a child.

No matter where your child is starting from, this book will show you how to help him or her build confidence and pursue what he or she considers most important.

Throughout this book, I share the approach to life that we teach at ConfidentLee® called A Confident Mindset™ (ACM).

ACM is a frame of mind. It is the outlook we want children to possess in the classroom, on the soccer field, at a music class, or while engaging in family activities. ACM provides a foundation:

- ◆ That having a belief in one's abilities, embodying positive values, and having commitment can help anyone become confident,
- ◆ That becoming confident is a step-by-step process,
- ◆ That living with a "why not" attitude and seizing opportunities can unlock a person's full potential.

The Power of Why Not is about instilling confidence in children that will lead them to say "yes" to opportunities in education, sports, or after-school activities. With this awareness, they learn that the outcome of success or failure is not what builds confidence. Instead, personal growth comes from the actions of practice and finding fun in all that they do.

HOW TO USE THIS BOOK

The ConfidentLee® program is available through various channels. It is taught by our talented team at ConfidentLee® in small group settings. It is also taught in classrooms as part of the school day.

At this point you may be wondering what to do if there is not such a program offered in your area or at the school the child attends does not offer such a program either. How can you develop confidence in a child you care about?

The Power of Why Not is not only for you but also about you, as the well-meaning adult involved in instilling a mindset of confidence in a child regardless of your own level of confidence. The book will provide you with our tried and tested methods so you can help the child be the best and most confident version of him or herself. With this mindset, a child will learn how to face fears and explore the opportunities in life by executing the power of why not. A Confident Mindset™ (ACM) helps children become school-ready and life-ready.

You realize the benefits of confidence building but may feel unsure of your ability to replicate what our trained team does for our students or educators in their classroom after receiving professional development.

I realize that classroom teaching has its advantages such as training and structured lessons, but being the adult in a child's life whom they trust and believe gives you a tremendous advantage. You know the child best and you can reinforce these skills in his or her daily life.

We recommend families with children in the same age group partner with each other using this book as a guide.

The Power of Why Not is organized into three parts and ten chapters:

Part I: Why Not is about why I believe confidence education is critical for a child's success. I share my own personal and professional experiences and hardships; what I have learned from well-meaning adults and the observations I've made in the classroom as a confidence educator.

Part II: Confidence Is Process-Based outlines confidence as a mindset that can be instilled and not just a skill set to be taught. I take you inside the classroom to share how we do it.

Part III: Your ACM Tool Kit is a step-by-step guide. It is a compilation of all my experiences, best practices, and frameworks I've gathered and created over the years that you can apply in real-life situations with the children you support and help.

While I hope this book will be helpful, I am not suggesting that, after performing the exercises, a child will have absolute confidence. That is not realistic. A child might struggle with the process, at times. Yet, instilling confidence in a child is an important and worthy pursuit for you, the well-meaning adult. It's possible you too might become discouraged. When you do, it's important to remind yourself confidence building is a process. Just like following a recipe, you're giving children the foundation to bolster their success in life. *The Power of Why Not* can be used as an empowering guide you can return to as you help children to choose "why not" instead of "why" in their everyday lives. I encourage you to reread and review chapters whenever you need encouragement to reinforce a concept. There is no greater gift you can give a child than a mindset of confidence. It will change his or her perspective on all things in the world.

My passion is to inform, educate, and develop confidence in children around the world. I want to start a movement for confidence education so that, before children are taught to read or write, they are taught how to become confident. To bolster this movement, I'm offering free resources to supplement this guide at www.namitaprasad.com.

Keeping a journal can be very helpful to children. There is a free e-journal for children available to download at www.namitaprasad.com. I encourage you to help your child get started using it. In Part III of the book, this journal will be especially helpful as you use the step-by-step processes.

I'm compelled to point out a caveat. Once you empower a child to become confident and to choose "why not," he or she might call you out if you choose otherwise. I share this from my personal experience as a mother to three kids. This has happened to me; it will perhaps happen to you as well. Instilling confidence in a child might affect your personal confidence as well. That's not the intention of the book, but it is often an outcome. The tools outlined in this book might even increase the confidence level of a family unit, team, or classroom by having a unified mindset of confidence.

Now that you have been forewarned, let us begin this journey. From one well-intentioned adult to another, my hope is for *The Power of Why Not* to be a useful resource and guide in helping you build confidence in a child.

PART I

✦

WHY NOT

PART I: STARTING POINT

In Part I, I explain why I believe confidence education is critical for a child's success. To do this, I take you through the challenges I faced during my confidence journey from youth to adulthood. I also share what I've learned from well-meaning adults, professional experiences, and the observations I've made in the classroom as a confidence educator.

CHAPTER 1

MY "WHY NOT" STORY

My mother enrolled me in a vocal music class when I was in second grade. Her friend, a musician, was teaching it and my mother felt she was helping both her friend and her child by signing me up.

"Namita, let's try to sing this chorus together. It'll be fun," said Ms. Monica.

It was the very first class and my first response was, "I don't think I can."

"Why do you say that?" asked Ms. Monica.

"I won't be any good at it. I am not a singer," I responded.

She looked at me with an assuring face. "Be confident. You can do it." She thought she was reassuring me; instead, she had me puzzled.

I tilted my head sideways and my little brain said, "But, how? How am I supposed to be confident? I don't know if I am any good at singing?" At home when my mother asked me how things went at the class, I got a bit upset. "Why do I have to learn singing?" My mother was taken aback. "Monica is a good teacher, what is making you so upset?""She asked me to be confident, and I don't even know if I have the voice to sing! How am I supposed to be confident?" Before Mom could say anything my father, or Pops as I call him, responded, "You do not need to be confident to learn singing. All you need to know is that you must show up to class and practice. It is practice that will help you become confident."

The first time I heard those words as a kid, I did not know what they meant.

"How do I become confident, Pops? Wow! You mean I can become a confident singer. You've heard me hum a few tunes; I am not that good." We both broke out into laughter. Apparently, I wasn't that good.

Pops, a man of few words, would say a lot without saying too much. "You can become confident at anything that is important to you."

"How, Pops?"

"Be brave. Be good. Work hard. Find fun. Be happy."

It was the first but not the last time I heard these words. I began calling them Pops' mantra to confidence.

That was easy for Pops to say; after all, he was a soldier in the Indian Army. I always saw him leading others. He was a good team player, both as a soldier and a devoted father.

"Pops, why does that lead to confidence?" It didn't seem as simple as he made it sound.

"Namita, when you are brave, you give things a shot. When you have good values, you make good choices in your actions. When you work hard, you become better. However, you will only work hard if you can find some fun in it. When you're working hard and finding fun, you'll make progress. With this progress, you'll become confident.

Confidence, to me, as a child was confusing. Some people around me construed it as some sort of mystical power that someone is either born with or has bestowed upon them.

They expected me *to be* confident. Yet, Pops kept telling me at every juncture of life that I could or would become confident.

I wished everyone around me had the same point of view on confidence.

Pops, a great mentor, would provide me with pieces, but also encouraged me to put the puzzle pieces together myself. Throughout my childhood, I learned to develop confidence by relying on his mantra.

New Kid in Town, New Things to Learn

Being a military family meant that every time Pops was transferred to a new base, the entire family also moved with him. For me, that meant every two to three years I had to quickly learn how to make new friends and establish new relationships with the adult influences in my life.

It's no simple task for anyone to start over so frequently, especially during their formative years. I wasn't the kid who was great at meeting new people. Constantly moving to different cities and schools wasn't easy. Even as a young child, Pops expected me to find my way in a new town. As a kid, that seemed like a tall task.

I would say, "Pops, I don't feel confident enough to meet new people. We just got into town. I don't know anybody."

"Namita, meeting new people doesn't require you to be confident upfront. It's about finding the courage each day to introduce yourself to at least one person. Be likable, so people want to get to know you better. Meeting new people is fun, you know. If you choose to, you can find fun in doing so. It will make you enjoy the process of meeting new people. Take notes. Jot down on a piece of paper the names of all the people you have introduced yourself to. I bet by the end of the week, you won't be the new kid in town anymore. You'll have seven new friends. I am sure that will make you happy."

When Pops addressed me by my name, I knew he was being serious.

I remember processing this advice in my mind: So, I don't have to be confident? All I need is the courage to meet new people? I can handle that! It took the pressure off me having to "be confident" from the get-go. Why did Pops need me to jot down who I was meeting? Was it because he thought I would forget or to make sure I was following through? I didn't know the answer, I just did it. (I wasn't aware then that I was keeping a journal.)

As Pops recommended, I introduced myself to at least one new person, and sometimes more than one, each day. It wasn't easy. I would get nervous at times. I shared that with Pops.

"So, are you afraid of meeting new people or nervous?"

"What's the difference Pops?"

"It means you are either scared that they might harm you or are nervous because you don't know them" asked Pops.

"Maybe a bit of both," I responded.

"Namita, if you're afraid because you sense danger then do not do so and let your mother or me know. However, if you are nervous take some deep breaths before you go up to someone. Breathing will calm your nerves."

Pops went on to teaching me some breathing exercises that I used throughout my life. I did as he advised. The next time I was nervous I practiced the simple breathing exercises Pops had taught me; it had a tremendous calming effect on me. I also began to find fun with breathing exercises and greetings. When I was practicing breathing, I imagined either smelling a flower or blowing out the candles on my birthday cake.

I also started asking everyone what their favorite color was and why. People loved talking about that kind of stuff. I had fun hearing their stories and would write down their name and favorite color and ended up using this as a memory game to see if I could recall their names and favorite colors. Sometimes I made up my own stories about why people had chosen certain colors and often caught myself giggling with the stories I fabricated. Making it fun made me want to do it more. By the end of each week, I met far more than seven people. With each greeting, I became more comfortable meeting new people.

Not surprisingly, repeatedly taking action to meet people instilled confidence in me. With each new person I got to know, I felt more comfortable making introductions. I was happier in the new town than I thought I'd be. Being the new kid in town wasn't daunting anymore. I had learned how to become confident whenever I was going to be around new people.

At Sunday dinners, Pops would check in with me. "How are you doing practicing meeting one new person each day?"

Pops loved using the word "practice". To him constructive practice was more important than the outcome.

I couldn't wait to tell Pops how it went. "I was brave like you told me to be, Pops. It wasn't so bad. It was actually fun. And I met *way* more than seven people!" I pulled out the piece of paper where I had jotted down the names. I realized I needed to rely on this piece of paper—my improvised journal—to recall.

If Pops had asked me to meet seven new people that week, I think I would have felt overwhelmed. However, since Pops had broken down the expectation for me to make one daily introduction, meeting new people seemed doable. And, just as important, he always encouraged me to find fun.

If my journal entry had a day for which I hadn't met anyone, where I wasn't able to follow through, Pops would offer advice and, on those days, when I had overshot my daily goal, he would offer praise.

Being the new kid ended up being a bittersweet experience. Just when I'd make alliances with key people, whether a teacher or swim instructor or classmate, I'd have to start all over again in a new place. However, learning how to meet new people made every move easier.

Looking back, over time, I became better with every move.

It seemed the more I practiced, the better I got or perhaps my method of practicing improved. Practicing meeting people helped me every time I was the new kid in town.

With practice, you get better. And, when you get better, you develop confidence. The confidence I gained—which incidentally was out of sheer necessity—came from setting small daily goals, practicing, and finding fun. This experience also taught me an invaluable lesson on how to adapt and be flexible in the face of change.

As we moved to different cities throughout India and lived on various army bases, Pops would also suggest skills he wanted me to learn. In Bangalore, it was gardening. In Jodhpur, it was riding a bicycle. In Delhi, it was swimming. In Jaipur, it was badminton.

As a child, I found it annoying that I was constantly expected to learn new things. I struggled with learning badminton. One day, I remember telling Pops I wanted to quit because I wasn't improving. I wasn't confident on the court.

"Namita, how are you feeling right now?" asked Pops.

Pops would always ask me how I was feeling in the moment, and I knew he was ascertaining if I was ready to receive his advice.

"Unsure," I responded.

"I don't care if you win. I don't care if you lose. Just getting on the court is already being brave. But you can't get better if you don't practice. So, let's just focus on the practice. Take a few minutes to write down how long you practiced, what you practiced, and how that affects your desire to play. Can you try that for a couple weeks?"

"I guess!" I shrugged my shoulders.

I took an old notebook and used crafts to make the cover of the notebook colorful. I would take a minute or two each day to write in it.

A few weeks later I knew I was getting better, but I still hadn't won a game. One day after another loss at badminton, Pops asked me, "How do you feel in this moment?" I looked at him surprised. I had just lost the game; how did he expect me to "feel?"

"Mad," I answered with a scowl.

"Don't be, I am proud of you. I have seen you practicing regularly."

I thought he was going to be upset but instead he was all smiles. I pulled out my notebook to show him. He looked over the notebook and praised me for sticking to practicing. Pops didn't care if I won or lost. My practice mattered to him the most.

He then asked me to think about how I could improve my practice. "Tell me in your opinion how your game can improve further."

"I guess I need to practice my serves."

"Let us practice together. How about we give different serves funny names so you can remember? I believe eventually, you'll become confident in your ability to serve."

Serve short became "serve shortie." Since I'm on the short side, this would make me giggle. I followed through with Pops' advice and continued to practice my serves. Somehow finding fun with the practice of serving and not worrying about the outcome made me want to practice more. Also, Pops wanted to make sure that the actions of practice did not have a negative connotation. He wanted me to enjoy practice.

As always, every time Pops had a teachable moment, he would gauge if I was open to receiving his advice. These check-ins became part of my childhood. He insisted that my reply only needed to be one word, no more, so I wouldn't overthink it.

With practice, my serving game had improved and my confidence in myself grew! I can't say I was ever good or that I won very many games, but I became skilled enough to play the game. This piqued my interest so much that I continued playing into adulthood.

Looking back, Pops didn't really care if I mastered any of these skill sets. He wanted me to understand that confidence building in badminton or anything for that matter was a process, regardless of what I learned. He also wanted me to have a record of my practice and then to self-reflect on the impact of this practice. To him it was the difference between intention and following through on practice. It was also the difference between practicing and taking the time to self-reflect on the actions of practice itself. Whether it's changing schools, making new friends, or learning how to serve in badminton, Pops was trying to help me understand that the path to learning included actions of practice, taking notes and tracking what I did. He believed it was also up to me to find the fun in the activity.

Some of my fondest memories were getting these pep talks from Pops. Each time I had to learn something new, I would ask him why. Pops would always give me a reassuring look and encourage me.

"Why not? Just give it a shot, Namita. If you practice, you will become confident." Why didn't he promise me success instead, just confidence? As a child I found his approach exasperating.

I often heard those words from Pops when I was unsure of myself. One day I asked Pops about his obsession with confidence.

"Pops, people always tell me to *be* confident. You tell me I will *become* confident. What's the difference?"

"Namita, there are times you'll be unsure of yourself, and you'll have to choose whether or not to give opportunities a shot. Anytime you feel stuck, remind yourself that you don't have to be confident before you begin something. You'll become confident through your actions of practice."

Whether I successfully learned what I was attempting wasn't as important. Frankly, he didn't care. It was the process of approaching opportunities that was his fixation.

Pops also never put pressure on me to be confident. His only expectation was for me to have courage, be a good kid, to practice, of course, he wanted me to find fun while doing all this. Although I didn't understand it back then, these defining moments would later shape my perspective on why confidence building is a step-by-step process and why the process was more important than the outcome itself. Though it was frustrating to me as a child, it was formative in shaping me into the person I am today. Once confidence became the end point and not the initial point, I learned to say "why not" to life's opportunities. To have the power and ability to take risks and make choices has been life-altering for me, as a woman, a single mother, and a professional.

Leading up to college, I attended several schools. The cities, schools, and the opportunities life presented me changed but Pops' advice did not.

Life Throws a Curveball

In 1987, Pops led his regiment overseas on a peacekeeping mission to Sri Lanka. During that time, I was a student at Lady Shri Ram College, New Delhi. Understanding the perils and the necessity for Pops' undertaking, I came home from college to say goodbye. As he left for duty, even in those moments of unnerving farewells, Pops still echoed the same sentiment.

"Why do you have to go?"

My question to him was answered by a simple, "Why not? It is my duty to my country."

Less than a year later, life threw me a curveball. In my second year of college, with no notice, my parents pulled me out of college and asked me to move to the U.S. to enter into an arranged marriage. What a punch to the gut! I was only eighteen-and-a-half and had intended to pursue higher education. It was a decision that would forever change the direction of my life. I was sad. I was confused. My mind was flooded with many "whys." This was the only time my parents wouldn't listen to my questioning their decision.

At that age, I couldn't stand up to Pops and Mom. Manish, my brother, resisted, but at twenty-two, he didn't have a voice either. To this day he regrets not going to bat harder for me. I regretted not standing up to my parents and choosing "why not." Why not let me continue my education?

When I stepped onto American soil, I knew I had an unknown future ahead of me. It was in that moment of time that Pops' mantra and teachable moments transformed into becoming the Confidence Mantra.

CONFIDENCE MANTRA
"Be brave. Be good. Work hard.
Find fun. Be happy."

Those were no longer going to be words that I heard Pops say to me. He wasn't around me anymore. Our interactions were through wispy blue aerograms and phone calls at momentous occasions.

Adopting the mantra to shape how I would approach my life as a young wife and an immigrant was the best tool I had.

Giving up my spot at Lady Shri Ram, my dream college, having my husband as my only safety net, being thousands of miles away from everything I knew, was a cultural and emotional shock. I began to navigate my way in a new country and my household with a man I had known for barely two weeks prior to marriage.

Despite the life transition, I was steadfast to complete my undergraduate studies. I wrote to Delhi University and discovered the school had a correspondence course through which I could complete the coursework for my undergraduate degree. I signed up and took my examinations at the Indian Embassy in Washington, DC. I was happy to receive an undergraduate degree.

Yet, it was heart-wrenching to receive a correspondence course bachelor's degree instead of a degree in Economics Honors from Lady Shri Ram College, New Delhi.

I decided to pursue a master's program. However, to my disappointment, the undergraduate degree I had received from the correspondence course was not recognized as a four-year degree in the United States. By then I also had familial responsibilities that became my priority. At age twenty-two, I was expecting a child.

My friends continued to get their MBAs, law degrees, and other advanced degrees; however, these options were no longer available to me.

I had taken a detour from my original educational goals so I could navigate this new life as a young wife and eventually a mother. I decided to approach life with the Confidence Mantra that I had learned early on as the new kid (or adult) in town or on the badminton court.

It helped me face the challenges of life.

As a new kid in town, it was about choosing why not and practicing making friends. On the badminton court it was about practicing irrespective of winning or losing. Now as an immigrant in a new country, it was about discovering ways to find a job. In the beginning, I felt a bit defeated. With my educational qualifications, I quickly realized that not only graduate programs, but job opportunities were limited. Realizing that I did not have the skill set to get a job, I once again leaned on the Confidence Mantra and decided to consider pursuing success in unconventional ways. I told myself that my best option of overcoming my lack of credentials was to change my professional pursuits.

I cannot say I wasn't upset with my parents for making the rash decision to pull me out of college and enter an arranged marriage. Why did they do this to me? Why did they disrupt my life?

Then one day it set in. I was in America! I was in the land of opportunity. It was time I apply the "why not" approach with which I was raised to my professional career.

Instead of trying to pursue higher education, becoming an entrepreneur felt like my only ticket to success. All I had to do was be brave and give entrepreneurship a chance.

Later in life, my parents admitted that they regretted the decision to disrupt my education.

"Why Not" Become an Entrepreneur?

My first entrepreneurial endeavor was in real estate at age nineteen. I saw an ad in the newspaper for a free real estate class. As a new immigrant, I had no clue what it was like to be a realtor in the United States. It was a free class and so I signed up for it. Soon after completing the class, I began working in the real estate industry.

With hard work, I found success in real estate. My real estate experience shaped my desire to work in a business that impacted people's lives. Helping people find a house of their dreams was gratifying to me. If it wasn't for the Confidence Mantra, that in turn instilled in me the power of why not, I might never have signed up in the first place.

I worked hard and diligently at learning how to be the best realtor I could be. I surrounded myself with experienced realtors to coach me. I took it as a blessing that I was helping families find the house of their dreams. With practice, my confidence in being a realtor increased and I became a top producing agent.

At the age of twenty-three I was happy to become a parent. I loved being in the real estate business, but I had personal goals to prioritize besides my professional goals. Being present for my daughter Karishma was one of them. I had my second child, my son Rohan, at age twenty-five. As a mother of two young children, I needed to have a schedule that could provide structure, support, and flexibility for me to be hands-on with Karishma and Rohan. The real estate business didn't allow me to do this. I told myself "why not" explore opportunities that would allow me to work and be available to my children.

My next career move was in the mortgage industry. To get into the house of their dreams, people need financing. I knew nothing about mortgage banking, but I relied on the Confidence Mantra once again. I told myself if I worked hard to learn, I could become confident at my job. My first boss and mentor, Mike Twigg, took a chance on me despite me having no prior experience in the industry. I began as a loan closer, working with attorneys and clients. Three months into my role, I made a mistake on a sizable loan. I was crestfallen that I had made a huge error that was going to cost the company money. Mike called me to his office. I was both afraid and nervous. I relied on breathing exercises; they had some effect on me but not a whole lot. I thought he was going to fire me, or at least hold me financially responsible. Instead, Mike gave me a talk, much like the ones I had with Pops when I was growing up.

"When you play, you make mistakes," Mike reassured me.

Unfortunately, that is not how I saw it. I straight away took the leap into negative self-talk and self-criticism. I poured out my fears to Mike.

"I am not capable of performing this job. I need to find another line of work."

Mike cut me off.

"I do not hire for job experience; I hire for attitude."

He continued, "I know you will learn on the job and make mistakes. I do not expect perfection. What I expect is progress. Go back and figure out why this happened and find ways for this not to happen again."

Mike took the time to help me dive deeper so I could self-reflect on what had happened. Still new in my role, I was overwhelmed with multiple closings at the end of the month. Instead of asking for help, I tried to do all the work myself and ended up messing up. I realized beating myself up or blaming the mistake on being overworked would not solve the problem. I learned a few things from that exchange:

- It's okay to ask for help.
- Choosing "why not" isn't always smooth sailing. Sometimes, it requires help and intervention from others.
- Seeking advice from people can help prevent problematic situations.

One of these go-to people in my life was Steve Lagana, the top producing loan originator. I closed many loans that Steve had originated. He was driven and cared about his customers. He took over for Mike Twigg. Under his leadership, I moved to loan processing. In this role, my work was customer facing, and I interacted heavily with realtors and insurance agents. For five years, I kept a 9-to-5 work schedule (or in my case, 8-to-4). I needed to be home every night to be hands-on with my little kids. Over time my skills at loan closing improved and I began training others.

Around this time, my marriage to Karishma and Rohan's father was collapsing. The realization set in that, if I got a divorce, I would have to be financially responsible not only for myself but also for my children. I liked my job at the mortgage company, but it wasn't financially sufficient to take care of a household. Once again, I had to rely on entrepreneurship. Even though there wasn't a particular business in which I was skilled I knew one thing for certain. I wanted to be in a business that impacted the lives of others.

I can do this, "why not", I told myself. The Confidence Mantra had taught me if I worked hard at something, I could become confident.

At the mortgage company, insurance agents often stopped by our office to solicit our clients who would need policies to protect their new homes. I was impressed by these insurance agents. They had businesses of their own where they were masters of their destinies. In conversations with them, I learned that their professional growth was based on sales and managing their teams. In my heart, I knew this kind of work might give me the financial independence I needed as a single mother.

I sought advice from Steve and shared my dreams of becoming a business owner in insurance and financial services. He encouraged me to build a community of people with whom I could surround myself to give me advice. The next time an insurance agent came to our office to solicit our business, I got the lowdown on how the agent started. I discovered that owning a business was a challenge and insurance sales were difficult. After all the investigating, I wasn't sure I was cut out to become an insurance business owner. I returned to Steve for more advice.

"If you don't believe in yourself, no one else will," Steve told me matter-of-factly. He encouraged me to repeat positive affirmations and to find the courage to give this opportunity that had presented itself to me a try.

Timely advice from people who want the best for you and believe in you can change your life. Steve's belief in my abilities helped me step outside my comfort zone. I began telling myself: I want to become a business owner someday—I can make it happen. Even though I don't have all the skills right now, I might be able to make it if I work hard. I surrounded myself with those who had the experience and asked them if they would be willing to mentor me.

Once I had my support group in place the Confidence Mantra helped me say "why not." And that is what I did.

I knew nothing about insurance and financial services, but I got into the business because I wanted to help people protect what was important to them and plan for their future. I studied diligently to get my licenses. I began calling companies from the yellow pages to get an interview with an insurance company. I got my first break from John G. Rogers of Nationwide Insurance.

As a newbie agent, I felt overwhelmed. In the beginning, I struggled to make my numbers. In fact, I had never really looked at my own insurance policy until I had to bring it in for a role-play session. The insurance business has the highest attrition rate. There were minimum quotas of sales to meet every week. Let's just say Sundays were not my favorite days. John was an excellent champion with sales and business leadership. I recall a time when I did not meet my sales goals and John asked what happened. My belief in myself was low after I didn't meet this challenge. I was brave, and I worked hard, just as Pops always told me to. Yet, my effort and actions were not leading to sales success. Pops said if I worked hard at something I would become confident; it certainly was not working this time. For a moment, I questioned Pops' mantra. I knew there were only so many chances I would get to meet my sales goals before I would be let go. I felt like a failure. I was the breadwinner for the family.

I remember going to John's office one day and breaking down. Yes, as you might guess, I took some deep breaths before entering his office. If there was a birthday cake in front me, I surely would have blown out all the candles. John helped me understand how to better strategize priorities with my team and reach the sales goals. In those days, cold calling and telemarketing were the way to make sales. Like many people, I did not like cold calling.

John told me there was no way out. "Practice making calls and each time you will get better at your cold-calling abilities. I know it's not fun, but it's up to you to find the fun in it."

Really, John? I asked myself. Find fun in cold calling? Even though he sounded a lot like Pops, I found myself saying, "You've got to be kidding."

At that moment, I could hear Pops' voice: Be good. Work hard. Find fun. Be happy. I was working hard, but I was not trying to find fun in my work. I knew then something had to be done differently.

Despite being discouraged, my team and I turned cold calling into a game. We set fun rewards for doing a certain number of cold callings. The rewards weren't monetary; rather, they were acts of service such as having a colleague take your automobile for a car wash or having them cook lunch. The moment we made it a game, we started enjoying the act of practicing cold calling. Once we made it fun, we practiced more. As I continued with this practice, much to my surprise (and John's) delight, my cold calling skills improved. As I got better, I saw my sales numbers progress. As I made sales through cold calling, my confidence in myself as an insurance agent also grew. Every time I helped a family protect their assets, be it a home or an auto, my confidence grew.

Once again, it was becoming apparent that confidence building was a process. The Confidence Mantra works, but I couldn't cherry-pick one part of it and expect the outcome of confidence. The mantra was a step-by-step process where each step was vital to building confidence. I'm forever grateful to John, not only for hiring me, but also for teaching me the importance of devising action plans and finding fun, no matter how difficult the task. I learned from him that you can control your actions, but not the outcome. He would say, "Sometimes you make progress and sometimes you don't. Get feedback, change the actions if needed, and get back at it."

With John as a guide, I excelled in my new endeavor. Our agency won many awards. A memorable champion, John's guidance propelled me on the path of business success.

I took time to self-reflect on this pivotal part of my life. I wondered if I hadn't had Mike, Steve, or John in my professional life, would I have been able to face challenges? Maybe, maybe not. What I internalized is that they were crucial for providing the guidance and support to help me achieve my goals. Pops will always be my lifelong guide and support, but I needed to surround myself with others as well.

Lacking Confidence as a Parent

For many years I was a single parent to Karishma and Rohan. With the best intentions, I remarried and moved to Michigan to start a new life. I also had to give up my insurance agency in Maryland that I had built one client at a time into a successful business and takeover a different agency in Michigan. I started navigating caring for a blended family; I now had three kids as my second husband had a child from a previous marriage. Soon, I realized the trials and tribulations of a blended family. I was in new surroundings, friends, business, and family. Within the first year, I could see that this union wasn't blossoming; however, I was adamant about doing my best to succeed in this marriage. The next few years were full of heartache and disappointment. It was one of the most difficult periods of my life.

I became pregnant and my marriage was unraveling. I was dealing with a blended family and now had a child on the way.

The marriage fell apart. I was heartbroken.

For decades, I had been building my confidence—often out of necessity—and bringing myself back to the Confidence Mantra which had now morphed into my own "why not" approach. Being a twice-divorced South Asian mother of three shook my self-belief and I felt like a failure—as a daughter, as a woman, and as a parent. I spent lots of days in negative "why me" self-talk about whether I was fit to be a mom and businesswoman.

By this time, I had a child in college, one in high school, and a toddler at home. I wanted to be strong for all of them, yet I couldn't. At times, I felt defeated and lost. I was down, overwhelmed, and didn't know what to do.

I did not regret the second marriage because I got the gift of my youngest daughter, Maahi. I found myself as a single mother once again, this time to three children.

Turning a Necessity into an Opportunity

I moved to a different city to get a fresh start on life. I didn't know anyone there. It took me back in time to when I was a little girl, moving to a new town. Being at the lowest point of confidence, I relied on the "why not" approach that was instilled in me as a child.

I stopped focusing on the parts of my life that didn't turn out as planned. Instead, I put my heart and soul into raising my kids and building my businesses. I decided to start each day with gratitude. I took some time to write down what I was grateful for. I used an old diary that I had. I found that living life with gratitude was slowly opening my mind to the prospect of brighter opportunities in life. Gratitude was building my belief in myself and helping me face my fears. On days where my mind would wander to the "why" instead of the "why not" I relied on reading this diary (journal) of gratitude to center myself. It became my very own personal tool to find my courage. When I found courage, my voice to myself took on a positive tone. I began to give myself positive self-affirmations. With this state of mind, I was able to open myself to opportunities.

It was during this time I grasped why it was imperative for Pops to teach me the process of how to become confident as a kid. Maybe he understood that life presents adults with difficult situations and the process of building confidence as a child can equip us to face fears and overcome challenges.

Pops was right. I had taken what he had taught me as a child and applied it to my personal and professional life as an adult.

Realizing the impact that Pops had on me, I wanted the same for my children. I was hands-on academically with Karishma and Rohan during their elementary and middle school years. I was committed to helping them achieve their personal dreams and discovered supplemental resources to teach them beyond their schoolwork. This helped me realize the importance of after-school learning.

By the time Maahi was in elementary school, there was no question I would enroll her in an after-school academic enrichment program. As I searched to find a suitable learning center for Maahi, I couldn't find one as child-centric as I wanted it to be. I leaned on my approach to life once again and thought, I should start my own. Why not?

I took it upon myself to dive deep into learning more about education and curriculum. I reached out to schoolteachers to help me understand how to mentor children. Entering the education field was a great fit, since I was a hands-on mother and a natural entrepreneur. Thanks to the support of my team at the insurance office, headed by Jeanette Oliva and Rose Accavitti, I ventured into the education field, intending to open an afterschool learning center. Jeanette became such an integral part of my life that I call her my life manager; office manager wasn't enough to describe her role in my life. Rose became my go-to person.

Her even-keeled disposition and positivity made it possible for me to branch out into my passion for working with children. My supportive team encouraged me to choose "why not."

As I began investigating different learning centers, I met Ajay Sunkara, who had established his own learning centers, and his right hand in operations, Hana Adas. I began investigating a few different education companies. The due diligence convinced me that Ajay had what it took to empower kids academically. With Ajay's help, I opened a learning center in Troy, Michigan.

I fell in love with helping children develop their academic prowess. My passion for enriching kids academically led me to open additional learning centers in surrounding areas. As the business grew, my friendship with Ajay and Hana also flourished. They became my sounding board and key people I added to my list of people who supported me.

Working with children at the learning center gave me insight into how they learn, think, and behave. It gave me the opportunity to see how some children were more successful than others when learning math and English. Their success wasn't based on their preexisting academic strengths. Often, the children who performed well weren't necessarily the ones who had spoken up in class; rather, it was those who showed up knowing that learning was a step-by-step process.

Observations at the Learning Center

As I worked with children at the learning centers, I observed three things that puzzled me:

1. During the assessment for enrollment, parents would see that their child was nervous and tell him or her to "be confident." I wondered how this was possible for the child when they had no clue what was on the placement test.

2. Most parents correlated the child's ability to speak in public with being confident. I often heard, "My child is confident; he

is comfortable speaking in front of others." They perceived the kid who could communicate with others as being confident.

3. Parents put more emphasis on the outcome of learning rather than the actions of practice.

As a child, I was confused about the origin of confidence, so I wasn't surprised to learn that my students and their parents were confused as well.

I sought Pops for advice on this.

A Father's Gift

Not only was Pops a soldier, but he was also an educator. After retiring from the Indian Army, Pops earned a bachelor's and a master's degree and ended up teaching Spanish at Bharatiya Vidya Bhavan in New Delhi. He had an affinity for language, but when he proposed to do so, it surprised me. I remember asking him why he made such a pivot in his life from war hero to Spanish educator. I got the usual response from Pops: "Why not?"

Pops ended up teaching Spanish for nineteen years. Each year, he got better at Spanish. From being the oldest student in his class to becoming a leading translator of Spanish in India, practice fueled Pops' confidence. He was the happiest retired person I have ever known. He loved to teach and enrich his students' lives.

This time around, when I wanted to ask Pops for advice, I couldn't. For the first time in my life, my father could not give me advice. At that point, unbeknownst to him and my family, he had developed symptoms of Alzheimer's disease. Left with no choice, I tried to decipher Pops' words of wisdom by unwrapping the gift of his mantra.

That's when I realized how to "become confident" wasn't just a Confidence Mantra; it was a timeless mindset for life itself. The key to confidence extended far beyond those two words. His mantra had served as a beacon to help me become confident. Somehow, he believed

I would ultimately become a happier person using the same approach he had towards his life, both in war and in peace. He also believed that choosing "why not" would unlock my potential for future success. Pops knew war wasn't just on the battlefield; life was full of little wars. But I didn't figure this out right away. I had to go through life's ups and downs to grasp the depth of these two words.

Learning how to become confident has had a profound effect on me as a woman, a professional, and a single mom. That's when my vision became clear. If confidence is the vessel to prepare children for a life of happiness and success, then I must share this vision with everyone. I began having discussions with the parents who brought their children to the academic learning centers. It turned out, this ideology of instilling confidence in children resonated with others as well. They, too, wanted their children to become confident and ultimately for them to be happy in life.

As I reflect on my childhood, I realize how Pops didn't lose any opportunity to send the crucial message of how to "become confident" to me. I have relied on his approach and attitude towards becoming confident at every age and stage of my life. Today, I can say with absolute certainty that knowing the process to become confident in any situation has changed the trajectory of my life. When I have temporarily lost confidence, I have relied on my support system to help me harness the power of "why not."

The philosopher Rumi said, "What you seek is seeking you." This applies to my life. I was seeking to become confident, which grew into my calling as a self-proclaimed confidence educator. And, since you are seeking a resource to help build confidence in a child, this book has found its way to you.

Key Points

- When children are brave, they give things a shot. When they have good values, they make good choices. When they practice, they improve.

- When children witness the progress that comes from practice, they develop confidence. Confidence can be gained from the commitment to the actions of practice.

- Motivation to practice, no matter how undesirable the task, comes from having the ability to find fun in practice.

- Surrounding oneself with people who support you and give you feedback can encourage you to choose "why not" to opportunities.

- A child who embraces confidence as a process can cross the bridge from "why" to "why not."

- The Confidence Mantra is a timeless mindset and an approach for life itself.

CHAPTER 2

"WHY NOT" UNDERSTAND CONFIDENCE

From the outset of my confidence education journey, I've posed a question to well-meaning adults (parents, educators, and other adults who have an influence over a child's life): "What does confidence mean to you when it comes to a child?" Over the years, I have received a variety of responses. These are examples of real responses I've received.

From a parent: "We'd like our daughter to speak up in front of other people. At home, she has no trouble opening up. But when in front of a group of people, she won't share her thoughts. For example, she's great at math, but her teacher says she won't raise her hand or take part in class discussions. I think she could use some confidence to speak up in class."

From a teacher: "I've got this great kid in class. He cares about the environment and wants to raise awareness about recycling. In class, he has no problem sharing his passion about the environment with a few friends. However, as great as his ideas are, he won't share them widely with the larger group because he tells me he gets nervous speaking in public. Sounds like he needs some confidence."

From an afterschool enrichment provider: "My student is afraid of trying new things. She can speak up. She loves drama. But she is afraid to try out. I wish she'd believe in herself more and be confident enough to audition. Also, if someone suggests she tries a different approach, she has a tough time accepting feedback. I wonder if that's why she doesn't want to try out for any kind of performance. I'd love for your program to give her the confidence to try things without worrying about the outcome."

From these and many conversations I've had with adults, I've uncovered a few conflicting interpretations of confidence:

- ✦ public speaking is the equivalent of having confidence
- ✦ introverted children aren't confident
- ✦ children who lack confidence aren't willing to try new things.

After talking to well-meaning adults, this confirmed for me that my understanding of confidence differed from that of other people. Parents, educators, and after-school program providers wanted children to possess confidence, but each of them had their own definition of confidence.

I also realized that most people believed that having the ability to speak publicly or be able to speak up meant a child was confident.

I wondered how children could possibly understand the meaning of confidence when everyone around them had a different definition in mind.

This is how I view confidence.

Confidence is a Mindset. Confidence is an approach to life and acquiring it is a process. Confidence is not a skill set; it's a mindset. This mindset applies whether you are trying something new or doing a simple part of your daily routine. By internalizing this reality, a child can learn any skill set.

Confidence is Teachable. No one is born confident. I wasn't. You weren't. Neither is a child. However, a well-meaning adult can guide a child through the process of building confidence. As a result, any child can become confident.

Confidence is not Public Speaking: Public speaking is a vital skill in life; it's a skill set. Confidence is an approach to life; it's a mindset. If a child has a mindset of confidence, he or she can learn public speaking or any other skill.

Public Speaking and Confidence

I have always believed that public speaking *is* an essential life skill. It allows one to inform, persuade, and entertain. Above all, it is the ability to make connections with others. Public speaking is the art of communicating clearly and is a crucial skill in everyday life. However, confidence and public speaking are not the same thing. Confidence is an approach to life itself and public speaking is a vital skill that will help you in many situations.

My foray into public speaking started back in 1999 when I met a dynamic lady named Nilima Mehra. Mrs. Mehra is the director and producer of several South Asian television shows in the Washington, DC area. We had often run into each other at professional events. One day, Mrs. Mehra reached out and asked me to consider becoming a hostess on her show.

I was surprised that she'd asked me. I had no background in media. I had no formal training. So, I responded as anyone would in my position.

"Why me? I don't really think I am equipped to be a host, Mrs. Mehra."

"Namita, you are a pleasant person, communicate well, and can think on your feet."

"Come on, Namita. If you believe you can do it, you'll surely be able to. You'll practice and train with us. Remember, the more you host on television, the better you'll get. The better you get, the more confident you'll feel. Have fun with the guests you're interviewing. If you aren't having fun, neither will they nor will the audience."

I thought about what she'd said, and it seemed to align with the Confidence Mantra. I didn't need to feel confident before accepting her offer. I just needed to believe in the mantra and put it to use.

In the beginning, I was nervous about being watched by millions of viewers. I had to undergo rigorous training, which helped me face this fear. Mrs. Mehra was right. Pops was right. The more shows I hosted, the better I became. The better I became, the more confident I was in my abilities as a host. Practice built my confidence. My confidence journey as a television hostess started with the mantra once again.

Little did I know, the confidence developed from hosting on television also had a positive influence on my work and personal life. My business presentations became more effective. I increased my client base and became more successful. In my personal life, I began having deeper connections with my family and friends. This made me a happier person. None of this would have transpired if Mrs. Mehra hadn't come into my life as a champion.

But I got lucky. Pops taught me how to become confident and instilled in me the "why not" approach. I am fortunate that I have had people in my life who believe in me and are willing to champion for me. However, children shouldn't have to wait for fate or a stroke of luck to put someone in their lives to instill confidence. What if there was a systematic approach to learning to become confident? Would it lead to children becoming happier and successful? What if children were taught how to surround themselves with people who would support them in this journey? Would they be able to face their fears and believe in themselves?

I dove deeper into this topic. Drawing from my experiences as a television hostess, I created a curriculum for public speaking that engaged the child's mind before teaching the child the craft of speech writing and speech delivery.

However, I did not want to create a curriculum that just taught public speaking—a skill that most adults believed was important for children to possess. I wanted to first teach the child how to approach learning any aspect of public speaking with a "why not" approach.

I asked myself, what if I applied the Confidence Mantra "Be brave. Be good. Work hard. Find fun. Be happy" to teach public speaking? Of course, you know the answer. I said, "why not?" This led me to choose public speaking as the first skill set that I would teach as a conduit to teaching and sharing the Confidence Mantra. The goal was to instill a mindset of confidence even though the outcome was the ability to speak in public more comfortably.

Confident "Lee" is Born

In the spring of 2015, I started teaching confidence building by offering a public speaking course.

But I didn't want it to *just* be a speaking course or speech class. I wanted to teach children how to live life confidently and learn to do so early in their lives.

My creative mind, as usual, wandered. I'd often envision this cute mascot-like character with massive confidence inspiring and instilling confidence in children. Shortly after, our mascot Lee was born, and what followed was the business name ConfidentLee®.

We started off by asking children questions about their fears:

+ What's getting in the way of having courage to speak in front of others?
+ What fears do you have?
+ Are you willing to embody positive character traits in class such as being good to yourself and to others?
+ Are you willing to perform the necessary practice required for presenting a speech?
+ Are you willing to find fun in speech practice?
+ Are you open to learning how to overcome challenges and the possibility of making mistakes and facing failure?

+ Are you willing to help each other with peer reviews?
+ Are you willing to self-reflect on how you can improve?
+ Are you open to feedback from your instructors and peers?

Sometimes I caught myself sounding like Pops when working with the students. In the classroom, somehow the intensity of these conversations peeled layers which exposed vulnerabilities and any underlying fears that the students had. I began to see transformations.

Although at that time I didn't have a formal framework created, there were key components to teaching confidence building that were becoming apparent. I was overwhelmed to see what was transpiring. The children were engaging in meaningful, put-your-guard-down conversations. It was a signal to me that I needed to create a confidence building curriculum.

I wanted to start a movement for confidence education. I knew Pops had given me the foundation of what confidence is and I had practiced living my life with that mindset. However, my background was in insurance and financial services, not in education. To create a structure to teach confidence building I would need to surround myself with others who did have experience working with kids. I began building a team at ConfidentLee®. Some team members helped me develop the program and others to teach it. I brought on certified teachers to help create a program. The instructors at ConfidentLee® are called Confidence Creators.

One of the instructors we were lucky to have on our team was Ms. JoAnn, who joined this journey early on as a Confidence Creator. Her passion and creativity were evident to all the students and their parents. I will take you into the classroom of Ms. JoAnn, where she is teaching students how to approach public speaking with a mindset of confidence. I will share with you the stories of three students, Kiara, Charlie, and Raj.

Mindset and Skill Set

Here is a glimpse of what transpired in one of the public speaking classes. The purpose of this class was to teach children how to approach public speaking with a mindset of confidence. I will explain how Ms. JoAnn's students Kiara, Charlie, and Raj each experience a different journey. The story that follows is about Kiara, Charlie, and Raj and their individual transformations, working through a class that concluded with each student presenting a final speech.

COURAGE FOR KIARA

Kiara, a bright and talented third grader, had inhibitions about taking part in activities that required her to project her voice. She was vocal at home, but she had challenges speaking at science fairs or when called upon in class. She knew the subject, but she was fearful about speaking up. Her fears led her to engage in negative self-talk.

Ms. JoAnn knew that using public speaking techniques could be helpful, but possibly wouldn't address the very core of the issue: Kiara lacked courage. During her ConfidentLee® instructor training, we discuss that to instill courage, children must first have a belief in their abilities and face their fears. Every child has something he or she is good at; identifying those strengths is a great place to start.

In talking with Kiara's mother, Ms. JoAnn learned Kiara had been teased when she had made a mistake on a book report in third grade. It had a deep effect on her. She didn't believe she had anything worthwhile to say. Since that incident, she had developed a fear of speaking and began clamming up every time she had to talk in front of others.

During the second class, Ms. JoAnn noticed Kiara made extremely creative visual aids and, often, Kiara's peers would watch her in awe. Kiara's creativity inspired others to think outside the box. She began lending a hand to the others. Soon, helping her peers expanded Kiara's faith in herself. Ms. JoAnn complimented Kiara for demonstrating creativity and asked for permission to keep her visual aids so she could share them with future students.

Kiara beamed at the praise. She knew the praise was honest. She knew her creative skills were her strengths. Whether given by an instructor or a well-meaning adult, praise is only useful when deserved. Children know the difference between praise that's deserved versus unearned.

Kiara wasn't sure if she wanted to do a presentation on how to make creative visual aids because of her fear of presenting. However, getting validation from her instructor and peers on something she was so passionate about proved to be the catalyst. It also didn't hurt that she got to showcase her strengths. Even though her voice quivered, Kiara was excited to share with the class.

Kiara was proud of her accomplishment; her happiness was evident to everyone. Discovering her unique strength and receiving deserved praise encouraged her to believe in herself. Once this self-belief emanated inside her, Kiara replaced her negative self-talk with positive self-talk. This boosted Kiara's courage.

Ms. JoAnn asked Kiara if she'd be willing to give a brief talk to the class about how to make creative visual aids. Offering her peers suggestions on how to improve their visual aids opened Kiara's mind to receiving feedback on her speaking abilities.

This newfound courage helped Kiara battle the negative self-talk. Once Kiara developed the courage to give public speaking a shot, she put her heart and soul into practicing her speech just as she did with everything else.

I often wonder whether it was the voice projection exercises that gave her the courage to speak. Or was it believing in herself and facing her fears that helped her find the courage to speak? I'm inclined to believe that a combination of both influenced her confidence. However, I also know that believing in herself helped her speak up. Presenting in front of others enhanced her courage.

Kiara was being seen and heard, which gave her courage a boost. She already possessed good values that drove her actions to want to help her peers. She was also hardworking and committed to getting better. Finding her courage changed her attitude. Being able to use her strengths to help others and receive praise from her peers encouraged her to speak up.

As the course progressed, Kiara wasn't always confident with her public speaking.

However, I noticed that every class was increasing her courage to at least try to speak up. Discovering her strength as the class expert in visual aids along with regular practice boosted her confidence as a speaker.

CHARACTER FOR CHARLIE

Then there was Charlie. Charlie, like many other children, was nervous when speaking in front of others. His voice was barely audible, and he struggled with incorporating body language when he spoke. He would often feel a sense of frustration and failure.

One day, Charlie came to Ms. JoAnn asking for pointers on how to orchestrate gestures and move more comfortably during a presentation.

Ms. JoAnn asked the class for suggestions. "Well, I take hip-hop classes, Ms. JoAnn," Raj replied. "Every time I need to learn a new dance, the teacher matches each word to a step. Maybe we need a dance?"

Ms. JoAnn asked me for feedback. After hearing her, I had a light bulb moment. "I have an idea! What if we use dance moves to remember how to use body language in a speech just like Raj does in hip-hop?"

The students loved the idea so much we came up with a makeshift dance that I rolled out in the next class. It was as simple as "You, Me, This, That." The children would point to the audience, to themselves, to the left, and to the right. They were asked to use these dance moves as they spoke in accordance with the content of their speech. The idea was such a hit. Several kids squealed and burst out giggling as each of them took turns trying out the makeshift dance.

Meanwhile, I saw Charlie in the corner practicing. The first few times, he struggled to remember the moves. Every time he forgot a step, he would become more frustrated and make more mistakes. What I observed about Charlie was that he often went off on his own and isolated himself from peers. I noticed he was being hard on himself and not finding fun in his practice. It was as if he viewed learning and practicing the dance as a chore rather than a joyful activity.

Ms. JoAnn walked up to Charlie.

"Hello, Charlie! It might help to practice with others so you can help each other. Trust me, the moves will come easier if you go easy on yourself and enjoy spending time with others."

Charlie looked at Ms. JoAnn and then at Raj and Kiara, who were giggling as they did the dance. He walked over and joined them. Immediately, Charlie loosened up. Once he let go of his inhibitions, he started finding fun in his practice and began incorporating body language into his speech seamlessly.

We've found that building confidence in children requires them to practice. Finding an element of fun in practice keeps the practice going. Charlie had the courage to improve and was committed to practicing. Once Charlie began finding fun in practice, he made progress. Charlie's parents informed me he was always awaiting excitedly for the next class, even though he still had many public speaking skills to learn.

COMMITMENT FOR RAJ

A natural leader, Raj was viewed as being kind and supportive of others. From the onset of the program, Raj was a talker. Ms. JoAnn and some of his peers wondered why he even enrolled in this class, since he seemed to have no problems speaking up. "Namita, why is Raj in this class?" Ms. JoAnn asked me. In all our instructor trainings we share with our team, public speaking skills are not synonymous with confidence. Confidence is a mindset; public speaking is a skill set. Yet Ms. JoAnn was asking me this question. I knew that this differentiation was going to be an important part of my message.

"Now, Ms. JoAnn, Raj has wonderful communication skills. That is a skill set that proves to be beneficial in life. However, just because he can speak up doesn't mean he is confident in all things. Remember, in training we discussed that confidence is an approach to life; it is a mindset." The word "mindset" always makes my team spring back to the core teachings of ConfidentLee® instructor training. This was not the first time I had encountered such a question from an instructor.

In public speaking, we use tongue twisters to teach pronunciation and fluency. It wasn't surprising that Raj was willing to participate in reciting the tongue twisters. He found them to be hilarious and was quite good at them. However, Raj's tardiness and forgetfulness held him back from soaring in this course.

An integral part of the public speaking class is speech construction. Raj seemed to find this aspect challenging. Ms. JoAnn would always have to remind him to bring his speech and visual aids to class. Yet, he would forget to do so and would try to recraft it at the last minute while his classmates, who were prepared, were getting plenty of time to practice their speech. That's where Kiara and Raj bonded. She often helped him design last-minute visual aids, which wasn't his strong suit. Raj was encouraging and offered to help Kiara practice since speech delivery came easily to him.

What I observed in Raj: He had the courage to speak in front of others. He had positive character traits of kindness and helpfulness towards others. However, he did not embody positive qualities of organization and follow-through, which are just as crucial for developing confidence. Raj would need to continue to work on his commitment.

Interestingly, I noticed more improvement in Kiara as she consistently practiced her speech, compared to Raj, who had issues with follow-through.

CONFIDENCE BEFORE PUBLIC SPEAKING

All the students were working hard to practice for their final presentations. The final presentations were a success! The students did a wonderful job. Many parents and students noticed I was more emotional than usual, particularly Charlie's mom, who approached me after the presentations ended.

"I am so proud of Charlie," his mom shared with me. "Namita, this public speaking course was wonderful." Hearing this made me smile.

Charlie's mom continued, "Learning public speaking has made Charlie more confident. Don't you think so?"

I was taken aback by her question.

Then, the response just flowed from me quite seamlessly. "Learning any skill impacts confidence of a child. Yes, Charlie is a more confident public speaker. However, it is not public speaking that built Charlie's confidence. He followed the step-by-step approach we teach for building confidence in anything. And it starts with the mindset. From there, it took having courage, embodying good values, and making a concerted effort that made him confident. If Charlie continues using this approach, be it in public speaking or anything he chooses to learn, he can become confident in that skill."

As I blurted out this answer, I realized it wasn't Charlie's mom I was trying to convince. This message was for me to convey to all parents. No matter how many times I share that confidence is a mindset and public speaking is a skill set, I think of Pops and smile. I want parents to know that confidence is far more than public speaking. It isn't just engaging an audience; it is engaging one's mind to approach life itself differently.

Voice projection allowed others to hear the children clearly. But it was the courage to believe in themselves and to face fears that helped the children become confident as speakers.

Being helpful allowed them to make friends. Embodying good values—by being good to themselves and to others—helped them become confident in who they were.

Learning about speech delivery allowed them to present with better eye contact. But it was the commitment to the actions of practice that helped them become confident.

This "become confident" approach had infused a new thought process in the students. They learned that anything was possible with courage, character, and a commitment to practice.

I wasn't sure I had all the answers to help children become confident. But after the lessons I learned by teaching several of these classes, I knew I was on the right track.

I knew this method worked. The children's delivery of a perfect speech was not how I measured their success. Witnessing children learn how to overcome their inhibitions and become confident enough to try a new skill set, regardless of the outcome, was more important to me. Did they show the courage to give public speaking a try? Did they embody positive character traits towards others and themselves in class? Did they follow through with effort for actions of practice? Were they finding fun while practicing? They sure seemed like a happy bunch, most of the time. In my world, these are the things I'm looking for because they contribute to the process of building confidence.

I still remember standing in the hallway, watching these kids with pride and elation, with tears in my eyes. I was in awe of their individual transformations. Some viewed that final presentation as the completion of a course. To me, it was so much more. These students had made progress in their public speaking skills but, more importantly, they had made progress in developing the mindset of confidence. Each student had taken a personal journey among supportive peers. And the framework I had implemented, though undefined, was making a difference. I was thankful for my team of talented instructors. I was proud of my students and myself for having a dream and going after it.

My goal was for kids to believe in themselves and give a wholehearted attempt at building their confidence. Like my students, there were times I didn't believe in myself. My career in education has evolved by both design and happenstance. I don't have an education degree. I'm not a certified teacher. I am also not a psychologist. I have no credentials either before or after my name. I often say I am an accidental educator because I saw a gap in confidence building in education, and I wanted to close it. Like my students, I also had fears. One of my biggest fears was whether the program would be well received.

ConfidentLee® is based on observations and findings from the classroom. Though I had a tremendous fear of putting my work out there, my passion for spreading the importance of how to become confident was far greater. After seeing transformations in the classroom over the years, I decided to rely on the why not approach and start the movement for confidence education.

Key Points

- Confidence is a mindset.

- Confidence is teachable.

- With practice anyone can become a confident public speaker.

- Before teaching public speaking or any skill set, it's important to understand the process to building confidence.

CHAPTER 3

"WHY NOT" TAKES A CONFIDENT MINDSET

Charlie's mom gave me much to think about. It wasn't the first time I was confronted with the challenge to define confidence in my own words. It also wasn't the first time someone had expressed curiosity about how their child would develop confidence.

At ConfidentLee® we teach various skills such as public speaking, debate, and entrepreneurship. However, before introducing any skill, we first introduce the mindset of how to become confident.

The curriculum we created initially worked on the mindset of the child and then on the skill itself. I noticed that when a child approached a situation with the knowledge that he or she did not have to be confident but rather could become confident, it helped change the whys into why nots.

Our efforts showed that possessing courage, embodying positive character values, and having the commitment to practice were crucial components to developing a mindset of confidence. I wanted to give children the tools to choose "why not" so that they could unlock their full potential. To do so, there was a need for courage. For that, I first needed to teach children the importance of positive affirmations and equip them with strategies to overcome negative self-talk. I also needed to set a framework for instilling positive character values. Next, I needed to spread awareness that having the commitment to actions of practice was pivotal in developing confidence. Finally, I wanted the child to learn how to find a speckle of fun, no matter how mundane the practice might be. It is my belief that having the ability to find fun in practice will serve as the motivation to continue practicing. I wondered if this was possible for me to accomplish, and I could immediately hear myself say, why not?

Often, I would attend classes taught by our team and watch the progress of the students. Sometimes I would help in the class; other times, I would observe. At the final presentations, I was a spectator and quite possibly the most emotional person in the room. Slowly, I concluded that the students who possessed courage, character, and commitment made progress at learning any skill set (be it public speaking or another offering). These were "aha" moments for me. I realized the importance of prioritizing confidence education before teaching them any other skill.

As I created a formal curriculum for teaching this method, I revisited the definition of "confidence." Up to this point, I was clear that confidence is a mindset, is teachable, and is not to be confused with public speaking. However, I wanted to put into words what confidence means for a child, in a short and simple way that he or she could understand.

CONFIDENCE

Confidence is a feeling. However, it is not a feeling with which you start out. **Confidence is the feeling you gain after the actions of practice.**

Confidence cannot be lumped in with other skill sets. It is not a skill to teach; it is an approach to life itself. Having a mindset of confidence could impact the outcome of any skill set for any child.

I began having open discussions with parents, educators, and my team. Many of them used the terms "mindset" and "skill set" interchangeably when referring to confidence building. Why was this occurring? To me, the link and the differences between mindset and skill set were apparent and I had to find a way to make other people aware of the distinction.

MINDSET

A mindset is an individual's view, a unique lens, on the world around that person. Mindset is the attitude with which we approach situations in life. It is a state of mind based on personal beliefs. These beliefs guide our actions in life. Whether we believe we can or can't is a mindset. For example, how we think about setting and achieving goals and overcoming challenges to achieve these goals is a mindset. A child's mindset will guide their decision to explore activities like sports or music. **A mindset can be shaped.**

SKILL SET

A skill set is the set of skills that a person has developed to use in life. A skill set is the combination of knowledge and abilities that an individual has developed through life and work. Skill sets include those that are quantifiable, such as academic knowledge, music, dance, and martial arts.

They also include social and interpersonal skills, such as being able to make friends or work in a group.

For example, what a child learns after enrolling in sports becomes a skill set or when a child demonstrates kindness, it becomes part of his or her skill set. Soccer and kindness are both skills and can be taught. **A skill set can be learned.**

So, you might wonder, which one comes first? The mindset or skill set? Which one is more important?

Here is my answer: They are both equally important! I believe a starting point for developing any skill set is having the right mindset.

A mindset guides the choice of actions, while a skill set is the outcome of these actions.

Taking the time to reflect upon the actions of practice performed to learn a skill set can encourage a child to understand the importance of mindset. There is no clear beginning and end point.

Both mindset and skill set help develop a child's capabilities.

But what is evident is that a mindset has a profound effect on the choices that the child makes.

If mindset is so important, I felt compelled to answer, what is a mindset of confidence? I understood the outcome—if a child had a mindset of confidence, she would choose "why not." Most likely, she also would be aware that confidence building is a step-by-step process. I'm not claiming that without a certain mindset you cannot learn a skill set. What I am proposing is with the right mindset, learning any skill set can be a smoother and much easier process.

For example, we found some children were comfortable speaking in front of others while others had to work harder at developing their speaking skills. However, the children who were the most proficient speakers weren't always the former. Often, the ones who put in the most practice made more progress, which led them to become confident. This confirmed for me that confidence in public speaking isn't something you start out with; rather, it's an outcome of the actions of practice.

I decided to give this approach to life a designation: A Confident Mindset™.

A CONFIDENT MINDSET™ (ACM)

ACM describes a frame of mind that possesses courage, character, and commitment. People with this thought process believe in themselves and face fears. They understand that having courage is the first step. The next step is to embody positive values that guide their commitment to actions of practice. They find fun and enjoyment in the actions of practice, which motivates them to commit to practice. When they confront challenges they reach out to peers for feedback. They are open to changing their practice based on the feedback. They understand confidence building is a process and this understanding empowers them to choose "why not." They embrace and persist through obstacles by self-reflection and feedback. ACM paves the path for a happy, fulfilling, and successful life.

3c's of a Confident Mindset™

Courage, character, and commitment individually are powerful.

But when all three are combined, they can become a changemaker in one's perspective and handling of life itself.

I began thinking how courage, character, and commitment instills this mindset. The child needs courage to get started, to set a goal, and devise an action plan. The child needs positive character values to guide these actions. However, without practice on how to develop courage or how to possess and rely on positive character traits this mindset could not be instilled. Thus, the actions of practice seemed to impact both courage and character. I am often asked whether there is a magic formula for confidence building. There is no one-size-fits-all answer. However, if the 3C's were a formula for A Confident Mindset™ (ACM), it would be:

ACM = (Courage x Commitment) + (Character x Commitment)

3C'S OF A CONFIDENT MINDSET™

COURAGE

The first C, which stands for "courage," is believing in yourself and your abilities. Having courage does not mean a person is without fear; it means an individual is able to face fears.

CHARACTER

The second C, which stands for "character," refers to personal values. It's the inner compass that guides actions of practice, decisions, and judgments in life towards oneself and others. Embodying good values guides the actions of practice.

COMMITMENT

The third C, which stands for "commitment," is the effort to engage in practice. Regular practice leads to progress. Self-reflection and feedback help improve or better one's practice.

Without the encouragement of my team—which is comprised of those who worked for ConfidentLee®, the well-meaning adults, and the children who took our classes—I might not have taken the step to start a movement or even write this book. Surrounding myself with people who not only encouraged me but also helped me work through roadblocks was crucial in my journey.

I cannot stress enough how invaluable it has been to work closely with students and their families. I learn so much by observing and eliciting feedback about every single class from both the parents and students.

I am grateful for the feedback from well-intentioned adults because it informs us about changes in a child's behavior beyond the ConfidentLee® classroom. The student feedback also helps bring modifications and more engagement to the program.

The early supporters of A Confident Mindset™ became champions of the program. They shared our work with other parents and teachers. Their children have shared their ConfidentLee® experiences with peers. This support elevated and supported my approach to confidence education.

I realized that ConfidentLee® was no longer a confidence building curriculum but had evolved into a movement. A movement takes a team. I began assembling mine, including supportive people from my past ventures.

I felt elated I had created my own group of supportive individuals

Confidence Support System

One huge lesson I learned in doing this work: if adults need champions, so do kids. This was a necessary component to teaching confidence and has evolved into the work we do at ConfidentLee®.

To the parents and children we served, I was a champion and so were our instructors. My team and I were able to help children become a more confident version of themselves.

A child is often surrounded by well-meaning adults. These include parents, relatives, caregivers, teachers, etc. These well-meaning adults play an important role in a child's life, but their role could be different from another well-meaning adult. Some may encourage the child and give them feedback to help them achieve what is important to them. Others might be responsible for taking care of the child. We call these well-meaning adults either Champions or Rocks.

> ### CHAMPION
>
> A Champion is the person the child respects and trusts. They encourage children and give them feedback to help better their practice. Champions may be involved for a certain period of time or a specific purpose to impart information, knowledge, and direction that can change the course of a child's life.

Then, there are those well-meaning adults we need to provide structure and a foundation in a child's life. These people are a solid and stable presence that support a child throughout his or her life. Their journey with the child is long-term. We refer to them as Rocks. They, too, provide feedback; however, they are a constant in a child's life. In my life, my mother was my Rock and my father was my Champion.

> ### ROCK
>
> A Rock is involved in a child's life on a day-to-day basis. They take responsibility for the child. They provide feedback and encourage the child to practice.

Similarities Between Rocks and Champions

Role in a Child's Life:

- Both Rocks and Champions are well-meaning people in a child's life.
- Both Rocks and Champions want the child to become confident, unlock his or her full potential, and be kind, happy, and successful.
- Both Rocks and Champions encourage a child to pursue what is important to him or her.

When children know that they are not alone and that they are surrounded by well-meaning adults in the capacity of either a Rock or a Champion, they are better equipped to overcome obstacles that can interfere with their progress.

Differences Between Rocks and Champions

Time Period of Presence: A Rock is a constant presence in a child's life. A Champion may be present for a brief or extended period of time.

Degree of Responsibility: A Rock takes complete responsibility for the child. A Champion may or may not take responsibility for the child.

Ability to Give Feedback: A Rock may or may not give feedback. Sometimes the child may not be primed to receive feedback from the Rock. In contrast, a Champion gives feedback, and the child is often amenable to this feedback.

Child's Perspective: Sometimes the feedback of a Champion is better received than feedback from a Rock. This may occur because a Rock is a constant presence in a child's life. Even the best Rocks need Champions for children.

Parents, grandparents, and relatives can be Champions and/or Rocks depending on the nature of the relationship and situation. The journey of Rocks and Champions can change and evolve over time. We refer to this group of people as a Circle of Confidence.

CIRCLE OF CONFIDENCE

A collective group of Rocks and Champions who are involved in supporting and encouraging children to become more confident and successful in life make up the Circle of Confidence.

The Circle of Confidence is crucial for every child to have and to identify. If a child is struggling to become better at a skill and doesn't know who or how to ask for help, he or she may stumble blindly. Learning from a young age to identify Rocks and Champions and create a Circle of Confidence is a skill that can provide lifelong benefits. Knowing how to approach a member of the Circle of Confidence is invaluable.

Encouraging a child to form a Circle of Confidence, before he or she ever needs to rely on it, is imperative. This is how the child identifies people to reach out to before she needs to ask for help or guidance.

The Circle of Confidence is not confined to just children. Adults also need to surround themselves with people who have a collective vision to help children become confident. We call it the Community of Confidence. They say it takes a village to raise a child. I feel it takes a community of supportive individuals to encourage an adult to instill confidence in a child.

COMMUNITY OF CONFIDENCE

A collective group of people who are a resource and provide feedback and encouragement to well-meaning adults in their journey to instill confidence in a child.

I realized that to start a movement, I would need to make parents, teachers, coaches, and after-school enrichment providers aware of A Confident Mindset™. This would allow children to be surrounded by Champions and Rocks in school, sports, activities, and life and enable children to experience a cohesive environment in which to build their confidence.

I knew that the wizardry of A Confident Mindset™ needed to be shared.

Key Points

- Confidence is not a feeling with which you start; it's the outcome of the actions of practice.

- A mindset is an individual's view, an approach, a unique lens on the world around him or her. A skill set is the set of skills that a person has developed to use in life.

- A Confident Mindset™ (ACM) describes a frame of mind that possesses courage, character, and commitment.

- Courage, character, and commitment individually are powerful. But when all three are combined, they can be a changemaker in a child's perspective and his or her handling of life's challenges.

- If adults need champions, so do kids.

- Rocks are well-meaning adults who are constantly present in a child's life and can provide feedback. Champions are well-meaning adults who are present for a varying period of time whom the child respects and asks for feedback.

- A collective group of Rocks and Champions who are involved in supporting and encouraging children to become more confident and successful in life makes up the child's Circle of Confidence.

- A collective group of people who are a resource and provide feedback and encouragement to well-meaning adults in their journey to instill confidence in a child makes up the Community of Confidence.

PART II

CONFIDENCE IS PROCESS-BASED

PART II STARTING POINT

In Part II, I share the confidence-building framework I created for the classroom, A Confident Mindset™ (ACM). In each chapter, I break down the steps of ACM: The Need for Courage, The Purpose of Character, and The Power of Commitment.

CHAPTER 4

THE NEED FOR COURAGE

In this chapter, you'll learn about how we teach the need for courage in the ConfidentLee® classroom. Courage is the first step to building confidence.

WHAT IS COURAGE?

Courage is the quality that enables people to believe in themselves and face a difficulty or fear.

Courage allows people to act upon something, not because they are fearless, but because they are willing to face their fears. It's when a child says, "I'm not sure if I can do it, but I'll give it a shot."

Courage puts children on the path of exploration, regardless of the outcome. They know there is a risk. Rather than relying on the feeling of confidence before taking the first step, courage means they are willing to take a step toward it despite being fearful.

As Martin Luther King Jr. said, "You don't have to see the whole staircase, just the first step."

Courage is crucial because it's the first step to possessing ACM

THE FIRST C: COURAGE

Developing courage is a two-step process:

Step 1: Believe in Yourself: The child believes he or she has the capability to perform the actions of practice.

Step 2: Face Fears: The child understands he or she doesn't need to be fearless but needs to face his or her fears.

Why is courage needed for the initial step? When we're surrounded by uncertainty, we can become fearful of taking action. You cannot start the journey to becoming confident without first having the courage to open your mind to opportunities.

The Need for Courage

Not long after seeing the success that resulted from the public speaking classes, I added entrepreneurship to our course offerings. I found that parents are passionate about teaching entrepreneurship skills to young kids.

Entrepreneurship is one of my favorite courses for two key reasons:

- It's the perfect platform to teach children the importance of possessing courage, character, and the commitment to both,
- It's a skill set that's new to most children, therefore it provides a child the perfect opportunity to self-reflect on the journey of learning something new.

In this class each child formulates his or her own business idea. However, for me, their actual business idea is not as important as the knowledge the child gains about the importance and outcome of possessing ACM.

Kiara's mother called me, asking about the other classes we teach at ConfidentLee®.

"Namita, Raj's mom mentioned you teach entrepreneurship. I told Kiara that might be fun. She didn't know what entrepreneurship was and wasn't sure if she'd be any good at it. She's not interested in enrolling, but I want her to try it out. Any suggestions?"

"If you're able to stop by with Kiara, I'd love to catch up with her," I responded. We scheduled a meeting for the same day.

Phone calls like this are not an anomaly; they are quite the norm. Well-meaning adults want their children to explore new things because it can broaden their outlook. A child, however, needs to first believe in him or herself and then face his or her fears before being able to take advantage of these opportunities. Courage opens their minds to seize possibilities.

When the duo arrived, Kiara greeted me with a big smile. We caught up on things, like how her mom was teaching her to sew, schoolwork and sports. Kiara loved being creative and had really taken to sewing. She also enjoyed knitting. However, sewing is what excited her the most.

"Kiara, I remember the visual aids you made in public speaking class. You worked so hard on them. I still show them as an example to others. I can hardly wait to see what you will make with your sewing machine!"

"Me, too, Ms. Namita! I'm using old T-shirts to make handbags. I promise I'll stop by and show you."

To help a child believe in him or herself, well-meaning adults need to be keen observers of their strengths. "What are you going to do with all the items you sew?"

"Not sure," Kiara pondered. "Maybe give them as gifts?"

"Great idea, Kiara. Hmm…I wonder what else you can do with them?" I was encouraging Kiara to think of some other ideas.

"I'm not sure, Ms. Namita." I could tell the wheels were turning in Kiara's mind.

I continued to probe.

"How about selling some of these items? You could use the money earned to get more sewing stuff or things for yourself. You could also donate your earnings to help others."

Kiara's eyes lit up. "Really? I can do that?"

"Of course, that's what we teach in entrepreneurship class." By focusing on Kiara's strength, I was inching my way towards helping her believe in herself.

"Wow! But what if it doesn't sell? What if nobody wants to pay for anything I make? I'm still a beginner and not that good yet."

We all have fears like Kiara's. At some point in our lives, we've all wondered, why would someone want what I have to offer?

Kiara did not need to overcome her fear; she just needed to face it.

"Kiara, how do you know no one will buy from you if you don't try? And, if they don't, you can follow your original plan and give them as gifts."

Kiara let out a sigh of relief, knowing that either scenario could work in her favor, which helped her to take the next step.

"Okay, I think I'll give it a shot." Those words were magic to my ears.

I understand not all fears can be so simple to tackle. Before a well-meaning adult can help children find courage, there needs to be a safe environment where children can share their innermost fears.

Now let's take you inside an entrepreneurship class at ConfidentLee®.

"I am going to have you all answer in one word how you feel in this very moment," Ms. Erica instructed. "I'll go first: 'excited!'"

Kiara: "Happy."

Raj: "Tired."

Charlie: "Scared."

Using the ConfidentLee® One-Word Check-in is important for setting the stage to peel the layers and develop courage. The child must be willing to receive before an instructor can give.

Ms. Erica is our ConfidentLee® instructor, and you'll recognize returning students Kiara, Charlie, and Raj.

"Good morning, everyone. My name is Ms. Erica.

"We are going to first begin with the ConfidentLee® One-Word Check-in."

At the beginning of each class, our instructors ask all students just one question, such as, "In one word tell me how you are feeling at this very moment?"

The one-word check-in gauges how a child is processing the world around him or her at that point in time. This lets the instructor know if the child is willing and open to receiving information.

I encourage well-meaning adults to use the one-word check-in before confidence-building conversations or other meaningful conversations. It gives them insight to the child's state of mind.

Step 1: Believe in Yourself

We must first instill the children's belief in themselves if they are to have the courage needed to embark on the journey of confidence building. Having courage means they know they can do something or achieve a goal. Believing in oneself and one's abilities is the prerequisite to facing fears. If children are full of fear, self-doubt, or negative self-talk and don't believe in themselves, they cannot take the first step toward building confidence.

So, how do children learn to believe in themselves? Our first step in the entrepreneurship class is to encourage children to identify and discover their strengths. What do you believe you're good at? This requires introspection from a child with guidance from an adult.

"The goal of this class is for each of you to start your own business." Ms. Erica instructed.

"I want all of you to think about what you might be good at and what you enjoy doing. You could make something to sell or find a service to offer. This is your opportunity to explore your creativity. No matter what business idea you come up with, each one of you will face challenges.

Overcoming them will lead to personal growth. Remember, let's find fun as we are developing business ideas."

Ms. Erica emphasized the word *fun* because she knew it was important for the children to learn how to find fun in each step of the practice.

"Before we change the discussion to what the business should be, let's first think about the process of starting a business."

Ms. Erica cleared her throat as if it was an invitation for the children to clear their minds.

"Starting a business requires courage. You have all heard of this word, but, what does courage really mean? Courage means being brave enough to do something that you're unsure about. In this class it means to start a business."

"I know you might be afraid about becoming a first-time entrepreneur. It's okay to have fears. Being courageous can get you started regardless of these fears."

"How can someone be courageous? To be courageous requires you to discover your strengths and abilities.

"To do so let us start by discovering what you are you good at."

Ms. Erica asked Charlie to share, "Charlie, what are you good at doing?"

Charlie: "I don't know, Ms. Erica. I'm not really good at anything special."

Ms. Erica: "Everyone is good at something. How do you spend your time after you get home from school?"

Charlie: "I take care of Dosco, my dog, and Keekee, my cat. I love playing with them."

Ms. Erica: "Is that right, Charlie?"

Charlie: "Yeah, I'm pretty good with animals."

Ms. Erica: "That is wonderful. I have a dog and I'm always looking for someone to walk him or take care of him when I travel. You could think about that as a business idea."

Charlie: "Do you think I can do that?"

Ms. Erica: "Why not?"

Charlie: "But I'm just a kid. Won't my neighbors think I'm too young to care for their pets?"

Ms. Erica: "You won't know if you don't try, right?"

Charlie's face lit up. Discovering what he was good at gave him self-belief. Even though he didn't have a clear idea of how his love for pets would develop into a business idea, he needed to find the courage to get started.

Ms. Erica approached Raj next.

Ms. Erica: "What about you Raj?"

Raj: "I slept late, Ms. Erica. I am so sleepy."

Ms. Erica: "Well, we need you fully rested. Make sure you get a good night of sleep. What are you good at?"

Raj: "Nothing."

Ms. Erica: "Nothing?"

Raj: "Yes, nothing,"

She had him do other class exercises and postponed the discussion until he was ready to receive. The one-word check-in gave Ms. Erica a good indication that it would be better to wait and reengage Raj later.

Step 2: Face Fears

How does one deal with fear? We show children, through introspection and activities, they don't need to bridge the gap from fear to courage all at once. They do not need to overcome fear; they just need to learn how to face it and push past it to take action.

Ms. Erica knew that conversations about fears with students were necessary because they all had fears and she wanted to address them early on. Kiara feared no one would buy from her. Charlie feared he was too young for his neighbors to take him seriously. Raj feared he had no good business idea.

It was apparent that Kiara was more creative than she gave herself credit for. Yet, she wasn't sure if she could make a business out of her crafts since it was only a hobby.

Kiara: "Ms. Erica, is the stuff I'm making good enough to sell? No one is going to pay real money for what I'm selling."

Ms. Erica knew Kiara was engaging in negative self-talk. Something needed to be done to have her face her fears.

"I have an idea, Kiara. Why don't you get your parents permission to conduct a survey in your neighborhood? Why not show your crafts to neighbors and ask if they would consider buying from you? The survey will help you understand if you are creating something that is beautiful to you but perhaps not easy to sell. If so, you will at least know you can create. You can then possibly try something different. For example, you might love making handbags from old T-shirts, but if you find out that even though they are lovely you aren't selling them, you might consider putting your knitting skills to use and make knit hats. Take a piece of paper and write down what responses you get. Do not rely on memory. Writing down in a dairy or journal will help you."

In handling Kiara's question, Ms. Erica wanted to reinforce to the children how finding their courage could help them overcome negative self-talk and the fear of failure.

"Kiara, why don't you create a display board with items you've sewn that can be displayed and shared? You can use your creative skills to do so."

Suddenly, the project took on a joyful turn for Kiara. Her mind was focused on the craft board instead of worrying about selling her crafts. Ms. Erica wanted the children to have a positive attitude towards the actions of practice.

I am always pleased by how finding fun alleviates fears and increases motivation. That was probably why Pops was insistent that I find fun in whatever I did.

Ms. Erica continued. "I want you all to give your business ideas a shot. What's the worst that can happen if you try? What's the worst that can happen if you do not try?"

Kiara blurted out, "I will never know till I give something a try if it is going to work so why not just go for it?"

Ms. Erica: "Class, I know you all feel a bit overwhelmed, possibly even scared. Let us take a moment and practice some breathing exercises. The first step to achieving your goal of setting up a business is to believe in yourself. Once you do this, you are ready to face your fears. Sometimes our fears don't go away; we just learn how to face them."

(I must share that whenever I get to see children use breathing to calm their nerves, I see the little me in them and it puts the biggest smile on my face.)

After suggesting that Kiara focus on having fun with the demo board, Ms. Erica asked Charlie to write down all the services he could provide a pet owner. Then, she returned to Raj, who needed a little more guidance.

Ms. Erica: "Raj, what about you? What do you like to do in your spare time?"

Raj: "Watch TV."

Raj wasn't sharing too much, so Ms. Erica knew it would be like pulling teeth to get his answers.

Ms. Erica: "What do you like to watch on TV?"

Raj: "Food Network."

She needed to keep her eyes and ears open to discover the children's strengths. As the instructor, it took Ms. Erica courage to stay on course and continue to ask open-ended questions of Raj. She had empathy and was kind in her approach. She was committed to helping Raj find something that he loved.

Ms. Erica: "Raj, do you like to cook?" Finally, there was a spark in Raj's eyes."

Raj: "Yeah, I love to bake."

Parents often ask me why courage is the first step to building confidence in a child. My answer is simple: "The need for courage is to get the child started. Courage does not make children fearless; it is what makes them believe they can take the first step towards facing their fears."

Key Points:

- Courage is the quality that enables people to believe in themselves and face a difficulty or fear.

- Courage is needed because it is the first step towards becoming confident.

- Recognizing strengths and abilities fosters self-belief.

- Self-belief allows people to face their fears.

CHAPTER 5

THE PURPOSE OF CHARACTER

In the previous chapter, we discussed how Kiara, Charlie, and Raj needed courage to uncover possible business ideas. In this chapter, you'll learn why and how we teach the purpose of character in the ConfidentLee® classroom.

> ### WHAT IS CHARACTER?
> Character is having positive values that are recognized as the right thing to do for yourself and for others.

Children who experience courage are able to take the first step towards pursuing what's important to them. However, courage without character can lead to unfavorable outcomes. Character is not just embodying positive values towards others. Character is about possessing positive character values towards oneself as well.

Positive values are qualities recognized as the right thing to do. Positive values toward others include kindness, gratitude, and helpfulness. They are often viewed as how we are good to others. In contrast, positive values such as time management, self-control, and resilience can be viewed as how we are good to ourselves.

If a child helps an elderly neighbor in need, the child is demonstrating positive values toward others.

Likewise, when children have ten minutes of free time, their positive values towards themselves will determine whether they choose to watch television or clean a messy room.

Commitment, follow-through, willpower, and motivation are also positive values. However, when I created the framework for A Confident Mindset™, I intentionally separated commitment from character. As a parent, I've witnessed my own children struggle to stay motivated to practice or to have the willpower to achieve a goal. As an educator I have seen the same in the classroom. *A lack of commitment dulls the presence of courage and character.* The commitment to courage and character is pivotal to instilling confidence in children.

Even though I view commitment as a subset of character, I find it beneficial to give commitment its own identity in A Confident Mindset™ framework.

The Purpose of Character

THE SECOND C: CHARACTER

Practicing positive values builds character. There are two parts to building character:

Step 3: Be Good to Myself: The child has positive values towards himself that guides his actions.

Step 4: Be Good to Others: The child has positive values that guides her actions toward others.

Using the ACM framework, the second "C" encourages children to incorporate positive character values into action plans to achieve goals.

Be Good to Myself

Positive values such as curiosity, self-control, creativity, open-mindedness, and resilience can be viewed as being good to ourselves. These values give children the power to believe they can make good decisions for themselves.

What's an example of being good to yourself? I'll take you back to Ms. Erica's Entrepreneurship classroom to demonstrate this point.

Raj initially didn't think he had any special talent. He wondered how watching Food Network and baking would have anything to do with entrepreneurship. Seeing Raj struggle with this, Ms. Erica approached him.

Ms. Erica: "Raj, what do you like to bake?"

Raj: "Brownies. They are so good."

Ms. Erica: "What is your recipe?"

Raj: "Ms. Erica, these are my own recipes. People are always asking me for my secret ingredients. I will write down the recipe for you."

Kiara: "Ooh, can you make us some?"

Raj: "Maybe."

Ms. Erica urged Raj to consider writing a recipe book to sell as his business venture. Raj got excited.

Raj: "Wow! That's a great idea."

Raj loved to bake. The next day, Raj showed up with brownies. The class was delighted. But Raj was embarrassed. He was disorganized and with the best of intentions he would forget to write down the brownie recipe. As delicious as his baked goods were, he never seemed to have the recipe ready to share.

Be Good to Others

Positive character values that define how we treat and relate to others include kindness, responsibility, gratitude, and good etiquette. These character values, which we view as being good to and with others, can help children make friends, show empathy, and gain perspective. Positive character values are circular in nature. They are never-ending.

Back in the classroom, Ms. Erica was helping the children walk through another exercise.

"Class, now it's time to give your business a name," Ms. Erica instructed. "Let's start with Kiara's business. Does anyone have a suggestion?"

Raj raised his hand.

"Ms. Erica, what if Kiara named her business Woodhaven Crafts? We are neighbors and that's our subdivision name."

"That's a great idea, Raj!" Ms. Erica acknowledged, as Kiara furiously took notes.

"Charlie, do you have any suggestions for Kiara?"

"Woodhaven Crafts, no way, that is silly, and it isn't a good name for Kiara's business, Raj your idea is no good!" responded Charlie. "What if she sells in another neighborhood? I don't second Raj's suggestion."

Raj got red in the face. Ms. Erica stepped in.

"Charlie, I understand that being honest in our feedback is important. However, along with being honest we must be respectful of the opinion of others, even if you disagree with their suggestions. I understand what you are trying to say. Kiara might expand outside of her neighborhood and thus should not limit her business name. However, the way you expressed yourself was disrespectful. I understand it takes courage to give feedback but without being respectful your feedback will fall on deaf ears, even if it is in the other person's best interest. Charlie, you have great ideas. But being respectful and kind when giving feedback is how you can truly help someone."

"Before giving feedback think of something, they did well and share that with them before telling what they need to work on. It is called the Glow and Grow technique to do so. A Glow is a compliment, and a Grow is a suggestion for improvement. By offering a genuine compliment the receiver is more open to feedback. Let us use this technique to offer feedback."

Ms. Erica asked him to respond once again.

"That's a great idea, Raj." Charlie began his feedback with a positive comment this time around. "Kiara will probably sell in her neighborhood. But I think she should think about whether later she might sell outside the neighborhood too."

Ms. Erica looked towards Kiara for a response.

"You're both right!" said Kiara as she suddenly stood up from her seat. Seeing her excitement, Charlie continued with his feedback.

"Hey Kiara, want to be partners? We can go to Woodhaven and Stoney Creek and do surveys. I can carry your display board for you. We can ask people if they want to buy your crafts and if they need help with their pets. Wouldn't that be fun?"

In our years of teaching ConfidentLee®, we have realized that kindness creates deep bonds between children. It also gives children the courage to speak up. Kiara needed help to talk to neighbors, and Charlie needed affirmation for his business idea as well. Having a friend to do this with seemed to make it easier.

"These are all great ideas. I am sure you all can see that by using the Glow and Grow technique, the receiver is much more open to your suggestion." said Erica. "It's exciting we have all decided on a basic outline for a business idea."

Ms. Erica followed up on the students' progress in the next class. All the students had decided on their business names, and they were excited to share their choices with each other.

"Congratulations. You are inching towards setting up your businesses. Each day, we will take small steps to launch them."

Ms. Erica is correct. Most children who come to us do not know what entrepreneurship is, let alone how to set up a business. Breaking their goal down into small actionable steps helps them believe their goal can be achieved.

The idea of positive character values is not novel. It is not my discovery. All well-meaning adults want children to embody positive values. Positive values give courage direction helping a child make good choices.

Once a child has learned to show courage and character, the next priority is commitment. The child must show follow-through with that courage and must stick to the action plans he or she has chosen.

The last "C" of ACM, however, is one that cannot be added to Courage and Character; rather, it multiplies the sum of their effect.

In my view it is:

$$Courage \times Commitment$$
$$+$$
$$Character \times Commitment$$
$$and\ not,$$
$$Courage + Character + Commitment.$$

Courage and character, without commitment, are dreams and not goals.

Key Points

- Children who have courage are able to take the first step toward pursuing what's important to them.

- Courage without character can lead to unfavorable outcomes.

- Character is not just embodying positive values towards others. Character is about possessing positive character values towards oneself as well.

- Positive values such as gratitude, curiosity, self-control, creativity, open-mindedness, and resilience can be viewed as being good to ourselves.

- Positive character values that define how we treat and relate to others include kindness, accountability, and good etiquette.

- Courage and character without commitment are dreams, not goals.

CHAPTER 6

THE POWER OF COMMITMENT

We've already discussed how children can combine courage and character to perform actions of practice. However, without the commitment to practice, progress might not be as likely.

> ## WHAT IS COMMITMENT?
> ## Commitment is being dedicated
> ## to actions of practice.

Commitment means doing what needs to be done regardless of what else is going on in your life. All actions of practice require commitment.

Confidence is the outcome of actions of practice. If a child wants to become a skilled pianist, he must make a commitment to practice regularly. The commitment to practice results in progress, no matter how minute, and that instills confidence. It is not easy to instill commitment in a child. It takes a combined effort from all the well-meaning adults in a child's life. Encouraging the child to find fun in the action of practice is the biggest motivator. The third "C" of ACM encourages children to focus on the actions of practice to build confidence. Commitment is the glue that affixes courage and character to confidence.

The Power of Commitment

THE THIRD C: COMMITMENT

Commitment is empowered by practice, whether it be routine or reflective. Having commitment is to focus on these two actions of practice:

Step 5: Regular Practice: The child commits to the practice, as needed.

Step 6: Better Practice: The child commits to elevating her practice through self-reflection and getting feedback.

What are actions of practice? Actions of practice is the repetition of an activity regularly according to a plan. Practice is central to a child's life. Understanding the importance of effort and hard work is an essential part of the development of a child's level of confidence.

Practice is one of the most common words recited to a child.

"Go practice the piano."

"Go practice multiplication tables."

How many times have you spoken these words to a child at one point or another? As a fellow well-meaning adult, I know I have said these exact words time and time again. As a confidence educator, I've realized several things:

+ Every kid's method of practice differs from that of someone else.

+ Finding fun and joy in practice motivates a child to engage in regular practice.
+ Self-reflection and feedback help a child perform better practice.
+ Practice needs to be tracked.
+ Confidence isn't stagnant in any stage; it is progressive.

Charlie had the courage to try things and share his opinions. He made great connections with ease. He did not demonstrate empathy for others. He shared his opinions but often without concern about how others would receive it.

Regular Practice

For Raj's, business to succeed, it was important for him to remember to take time to write down his recipes as he baked.

For Kiara, it was crucial she shift her focus from worrying about whether anyone would buy her creations and instead enjoy the process of making the crafts she loved. I would often see her going through her notes from her survey. It made me realize that journaling can be used as a resource to have children self-reflect on their actions of practice, a vital step for continued progress.

For Charlie, it was important he learn to believe in himself, regardless of his age.

Giving children some control over their decisions makes it fun and less of a chore for them. This is how they find their internal drive to change their outcomes. Having this control can be transformative. Learning to be in charge of my actions of practice was an important life lesson for me. It came in handy when I had to accomplish business tasks or household tasks.

You might think: Really, Namita, good for you. But how do I get a child to do his math homework?

I get it. Math homework is not writing recipes. But it needs the same actions of practicing commitment. If the child doesn't have some level of control over his practice, he will not stick to it. Pops could have forced me to meet people in his presence, but he wanted me to do it on my own, not just when he was around. Ms. Erica could force Raj to write out the recipes in the class, but she wanted to instill the importance of follow-through.

Finding fun instills the joyful pursuit of practice. I know it is not easy, but it is vital to performing the actions of regular practice. When meeting new people became fun and when telemarketing became a game, I was more motivated to engage in the actions of practice.

Raj was aware that he needed to put together his recipes. At times he forgot he had to, at other times he told himself he would get to it later and never really did.

One day Raj showed up with a bunch of recipes written on stickies. Ms. Erica was pleasantly surprised. "Raj, this is wonderful. I am so proud of you!"

Raj's face showed that he was proud of himself as well. "I have to tell you, Ms. Erica. I called my Aunt Michelle, who is also a baker. We have baked several times together. She helped me."

"How did she help you, Raj?"

"She reminded me that whenever I bake with her, I bring colorful stickies and use them to take notes about ingredients. I have a corkboard in my room that is full of stickies. I have color-coded them. Cookies are yellow, cakes are red mostly because I love red velvet cake, and brownies are of course brown. I decided to do the same. I have packs of yellow, red, and brown stickies now in the kitchen right next to the baking stuff. Look, Ms. Erica, here are all my recipes." Raj proudly presented a bunch of stickies which had recipes written on them.

Finding fun using colorful stickies helped Raj stay motivated to write recipes.

Meanwhile, Kiara and Charlie had taken the time to go out and conduct a survey in the neighborhood. They decided to set aside an hour on Friday evenings and an hour on Saturday afternoons for a couple weeks to conduct surveys.

"Ms. Erica, guess what?"

"What is it, Charlie?"

"People actually want me to pet sit for them. Mr. Rogers has a surgery coming up and he wants me to start right away. I guess I am in business."

"How about your business, Kiara?"

"Some of the neighbors were interested in my stuff but something interesting came up. Mrs. Cassidy loved my crafts. She said she wanted me to make to a craft project for her granddaughter's birthday party. I guess I might become the activity for kids' birthday parties."

Ms. Erica smiled.

"Kiara, good for you. You discovered a different way to use your crafty side to develop a business. None of this would have happened if you did not have the courage and the commitment to conduct surveys. You are demonstrating positive character traits such as respect and etiquette. Otherwise, your neighbors would never offer you these opportunities. I am so proud of each of you. You are showing the commitment to perform actions of practice."

Better Practice

As important as it is to teach kids to stick to actions of practice, it is equally important to teach them when and how to elicit feedback from others to improve their practice. It is not just the actions of practice but the self-reflection of these that helps regular practice become better practice.

"Raj, how are you doing with the recipe book?"

Ms. Erica expected a different answer than what she received.

"I can't keep track of all these stickies. It worked for me when I baked with Aunt Michelle. I know they are color-coded, but I still cannot seem to figure out how to organize them. I try and then my mind goes into baking.

I find myself going online to find a different way to bake the same item. Then I find myself looking for baking videos. Sometimes I find other videos that interest me. Often, I end up being online longer than I had planned for. I am not able to stay on track and put my mind to organizing the recipes. How can I pull them together into a recipe book?"

Ms. Erica looked at the class for advice.

"Class, Raj is getting distracted and is finding it difficult to stay on track to create a recipe book. Any advice for him so he does not get distracted?"

Kiara raised her hand. "Ms. Erica, what is being distracted mean?"

"Good question, Kiara. To be distracted means not being able to stay on task. Raj knows he needs to write his recipes, but he gets distracted and is spending too much time online."

"Raj, I love to scrapbook. What if your recipe book was different? What if it was like a recipe book but more like a scrapbook? You can hot glue your stickies on. I will help you. It will be fun!"

"Great idea, Kiara. Geez, thanks!" Raj said, relieved.

"Good feedback, Kiara. Feedback doesn't always have to come from an adult; your peers can give you feedback as well. Scrapbooking might help. Try it out. It seems to me that you're distracted by something you truly love, which is baking."

Ms. Erica turned to Charlie. "How is the pet sitting business? Have you started helping Mr. Rogers?"

"I am helping Mr. Rogers," responded Charlie with a glum look on his face.

"What is going on, Charlie? Did Mr. Rogers cancel on you?"

"No, he did not. But I had to cancel on someone."

"What happened, Charlie?"

"I forgot that I had promised Mr. Rogers right when I was at his house conducting the survey. I forgot the date and promised another neighbor, Mrs. Connelly, as well. She was upset that I had to cancel on her."

"Charlie, I am happy to see that you are taking time to self-reflect on your actions. Here is a suggestion to overcome this challenge. Managing time is a common challenge that most business owners face. You could keep a calendar and write down when you promise someone a date. Why don't you go back to Mrs. Connelly and offer to watch her dog for free one evening as a way of apologizing for the inconvenience."

"You are right, Ms. Erica. I am going to use the money that Mr. Rogers paid me to buy a planner. I need to keep track of my school stuff and also soccer practice and games before I say yes to pet sitting."

Ms. Erica looked at the students.

"Students, I just offered Charlie feedback and I used the Glow and Grow technique to do so. I complimented Charlie that he is taking time to self-reflect on his actions and then I offered him feedback."

"Kiara, how about you, fill us in."

"Ms. Erica, I am still making my crafts. My mom has offered to help me set up a table one Sunday a month at the farmer's market. It will help me figure out if people want to buy what I am making. She said I can also do birthday parties as long as I keep my grades up."

As children reflect on their challenges, they can assess whether they require help from others or if they can overcome challenges on their own, or perhaps a combination of both. Depending on the child's assessment of their progress, they may choose to move ahead and get help to pursue their plans. Or, they may choose to step back and try another venture. That is also progress. It means they have considered the challenges and whether they want to move forward or change direction.

Self-reflection and getting feedback from their Circle of Confidence is crucial to ensuring progress. It lifts regular practice to better practice.

I've been throwing around the terms "regular practice" and "better practice" at you a lot. Now, I'll break it down further, as this is what the power of commitment is all about.

Regular Practice + Self-Reflection + Getting Feedback = Better Practice

Teaching children to have commitment is a daunting, yet doable task. Children learn more easily when they are having fun, which is why we incorporate all characteristics of play in our teaching. From the get-go, we have included enjoyable and lively activities in the ConfidentLee®

program to engage a child's brain. Children accept critical feedback better when they are having fun.

Practice is vital and cannot be overemphasized. Tracking practice is equally crucial. I believe that practice isn't what you do because you are confident; it's the thing that you do that makes you confident. I'm going to take you back into the ConfidentLee® classroom to show you how a champion can impart valuable advice.

Raj: "Ms. Erica, my grandpa is an entrepreneur. Can I bring him to class? He is visiting and I am sure he'd be willing to share his story."

"Certainly, Raj. Why not? What a great idea!" Ms. Erica knows children need a Circle of Confidence consisting of Champions and Rocks to support them. She had a feeling Grandpa John would be a valuable guest to invite to class.

Grandpa John visited the next class as a guest speaker and shared his entrepreneurial story. "I was sixteen when I started my very first business. My first business was building decks. My goal was very simple. I wanted to work for myself. But soon, I realized it wasn't easy. It never is. But it was one of the most rewarding things I've ever done. Every time I made a family happy because they had a beautiful outdoor space to play with their kids, entertain or just relax, it made me happy as well. Over time I started learning new skills and building more than decks. I became a contractor and later a builder. Today my company can build an entire home."

Grandpa John continued, having captivated the audience. "Entrepreneurship requires you to have courage to think outside the box. Entrepreneurs find solutions where others see problems. It takes belief in yourself, hard work, and persistence to get a business going. Along the way, you might face challenges. Sometimes, you might get discouraged or lose the motivation to keep going."

Grandpa John paused, allowing that thought to permeate throughout the class, which was so silent you could hear a pin drop. "In closing, I will say that you can set and achieve any goal with courage, determination, and guidance. Anything is possible if you have a belief in yourself."

The kids gave Grandpa John a roaring applause and then he asked the students if they had questions for him.

Ms. Erica knew that hearing about Grandpa John's personal story could give the class hope and courage. If the children could hear how a successful entrepreneur has faced challenges, made mistakes, and failed, they could feel inspired and encouraged to test their own boundaries too.

Raj had courage and character but needed to make a lot of improvement in his commitment and organization skills. Children who lack self-motivation to practice can rely on their Circle of Confidence.

Raj went up to Grandpa John. He explained his challenge to him.

Grandpa John congratulated him. "Good going, Raj."

Raj was confused; he had just presented a problem, but he was receiving praise.

"I am happy you are reaching out to others for help with your business," Grandpa John continued. "Not only business owners but everyone needs help from others."

Raj was relieved. He listened intently.

"Raj, what challenges are you facing?" Grandpa John asked and leaned in to listen.

Raj had tried several options including scrapbooking but wasn't really enjoying the creation of the recipe book.

"I love to bake," Raj responded immediately. "I thought about writing a cookbook as a business idea. However, baking is fun but writing a cookbook isn't."

"It is okay to change your business idea as long as you are not quitting and giving up," responded Grandpa John. "Ms. Erica says you have been trying different strategies. Let us go back and revisit your strengths. What else are you really good at?"

"I'm good at talking to people," Raj proudly admitted. "I can talk to anybody."

"Well, why don't you look for a partner? Find someone who you can help and who can help you." Grandpa John's advice echoed much of what we teach in our classrooms.

Kiara was listening intently. "Want to be my partner, Raj? I'm trying to get better at talking to people. You can come with me to the farmer's market. I know I could use help at the birthday parties."

Raj was excited that Kiara offered to partner with him. "Kiara, that'd be awesome! I love talking to new people. Maybe you can help me become more organized. I can help you set up your crafts for a sale." Kiara gave him a big smile. Organization was her strength.

Grandpa John addressed the class once again. "Your Circle of Confidence doesn't have to include only adults. It can include your peers as well. Kiara raised her hand. "Mr. Johnson, Raj and I are in each other's Circle of Confidence."

At ConfidentLee®, we call upon our students to give feedback to their peers. When two children engage in collaborative feedback, this way of communicating can benefit both the giver and receiver.

The child receiving feedback must listen intently to what the speaker is saying, thus building active listening skills. Learning how to give and receive feedback is how regular practice changes into better practice. We must also provide feedback in a helpful way. The feedback should focus on something specific and needs to be communicated in a positive way, so that the recipient doesn't feel he or she is being attacked.

Our program presents opportunities for instructors and peers to provide and receive feedback in the classroom, which enables individuals to serve as champions for each other. I hope to do the same for you in the last part of this book.

I don't believe one needs to reach a level of perfection to feel confident; however, I believe that having commitment to practicing builds confidence in any activity. Of course, being committed to practice one activity doesn't mean being obsessed with that activity to the point of ignoring other responsibilities or one's own well-being.

After better practice, two things usually happen.

1. Success
2. Identify areas for growth

Kiara's business took a turn from selling crafts to teaching craft activities at birthday parties. Raj decided to continue baking for fun. He joined Kiara's business as a partner. Charlie continued with his pet sitting business.

"Raj, what are your takeaways from learning entrepreneurship?"

"Ms. Erica, I think I learned that just because I love doing something, it does not mean it is going to be my career. I can do things that I love and I can find other things that I am good at."

"Raj, do not look at your baking business as a failure. You are more confident of yourself because you know your strengths and are aware of areas of growth."

Raj smiled.

"What about you, Charlie?"

"I know, Ms. Erica, you tell us to be good to ourselves and to others. I realized that I was being good to others and wanted to help everyone, but first I need to be good to myself and manage my time better."

"Good job, Charlie. You have a good heart, and you want to help others. That is wonderful. However, you must first organize your life and only then can you help others."

"And you, Kiara?"

"Ms. Erica, I need to believe in myself. I am always unsure. I realized that I need to give things a try. I am so glad Raj is partnering with me. I think it will be fun to do birthday parties together. My mom is happy too as his parents are willing to drive us as well."

Ms. Erica smiled. For her it wasn't the success of the businesses of her students that made teaching this class fulfilling. It was the small transformations that she saw in the children and their "aha" moments.

Success and identifying areas for growth are outcomes of practice. However, in each of these circumstances it isn't the outcome that builds confidence, it is the actions of practice itself.

Now that I've shared with you how confidence building is a step-by-step process and that these steps can be applied to any skill, the next section provides a confidence building tool kit to instill ACM in the children you support and help.

KEY POINTS

- Commitment is being dedicated to actions of practice. It means doing what is necessary.

- Children learn best when they know how to find fun in the practice no matter how minute or mundane it is.

- As children reflect on their challenges, through discussions with their parents, teachers, and friends, they can assess if they require help from others to overcome the challenge or whether they can resolve it on their own.

- Children also learn to distinguish between challenges and distractions.

- Understanding the importance of regular practice and elevating to better practice (with the help of their Circle of Confidence) is crucial to ensuring a child's progress.

- Children should engage in collaborative feedback, which can benefit both the giver and the receiver.

- Confidence comes from the actions of practice itself. Well-meaning adults need to help children process success and identify areas for growth.

PART III

✦

YOUR ACM TOOL KIT

PART III STARTING POINT

Think of Part III as your confidence building tool kit. In it you will find essential resources and tools to instill the three confidence building attributes (Courage, Character, and Commitment). Within each tool kit, there are explanations, examples, and exercises to practice the process of confidence building with children.

E-Journal and Exercises

Confidence building is a process any well-meaning adult can follow to instill confidence in a child. However, confidence building is truly a team sport. You, the well-meaning adult, and the child both need to engage in the process together. For this reason, I created this book as a resource for you, and an e-journal for the child.

As you read through this tool kit, you may come across an exercise we do in our classroom that makes you think I should try this! If you simply think about it, you may not remember to return to it. Even well-meaning adults have a multitude of thoughts on their mind at any given moment. They want to do their best for children, but life gets in the way. That's why I created the *E-Journal for Children*.

Use the e-journal as a tool to encourage purposeful conversations with the child.

Likewise, for children to develop their confidence, they need to dive deep within themselves with the support of a well-meaning adult. The children can use the e-journal to jot down their feelings as though they were talking to a friend.

I believe journaling is a powerful tool anyone can use to enhance their personal well-being. The child can write down thoughts, ideas, and "aha" moments.

Progress is the biggest source of inspiration for a child to continue to practice rather than live life on autopilot. When the journal serves as both confidante and guide, it becomes more than a journal. It is a record of their progress, and it becomes the catalyst for change.

This e-journal is an optional resource. Otherwise, you can simply have a conversation or grab a plain sheet of paper and follow along with the exercises in each of the following chapters. To download your free copy of the journal, visit **www.namitaprasad.com.**

Without further ado, let's get started.

3C'S OF
A CONFIDENT MINDSET™

| THE NEED FOR COURAGE | STEP 1 Believe in Yourself |
| | STEP 2 Face Fears |

✦ ✦ ✦

| THE PURPOSE OF CHARACTER | STEP 3 Be Good to Yourself |
| | STEP 4 Be Good to Others |

✦ ✦ ✦

| THE POWER OF COMMITMENT | STEP 5 Regular Practice |
| | STEP 6 Better Practice |

CHAPTER 7

GETTING STARTED

Before you jump right into the confidence building tool kits, let's review some concepts we've discussed so you're not using them willy-nilly.

How to Set the Stage for the Child

Before and after having any confidence building discussion with a child, the well-meaning adult will conduct a one-word check-in. We use this check-in tool in our classrooms. Pops used this tool with me, and as a mother, this tool has proven to be very beneficial for discussions with my children.

The one-word check-in helps set the stage for meaningful conversations. This is important because it gives the well-meaning adult an insight into how the child is processing the world around them. For example, a child who answers "stressed" might not be in the state of mind to dive into a deeper discussion. Confidence discussions are more advantageous when the child is on an even keel. If the child is emotional or tackling another issue, table this discussion for another day. This is especially imperative when giving feedback.

Exercise 1: One-Word Check-In

Start a conversation, grab a piece of paper, or download the *E-Journal for Children.*

Ask the child:
1.1 In one word, describe how are you feeling right now?

Explaining Confidence to a Child

The purpose of confidence education is for children to have awareness that confidence building is a process. Our goal is to help them understand what confidence is, what can get in the way, how to overcome challenges, how to self-reflect, and how to surround themselves with well-meaning people who will give them feedback.

As Rocks and/or Champions, we ourselves must first be clear about the meaning of confidence before we can set the expectation for the child. Explaining confidence as a mindset to a child may seem overwhelming, but it really isn't.

You need to convey to a child that confidence is simply an approach to any life situation and a way to go about doing things. Assure them that confidence doesn't happen overnight, and actions of practice take commitment. Each action of practice, as small as it may be, has an effect on confidence building. Discuss with the child what he or she learned from their actions of practice. By talking about the practice, the child is likely to realize the benefits of each step, even if things didn't go as smoothly as expected. Even though Raj did not follow through with his business plan, his confidence grew, nevertheless.

Encouraging children to savor the actions of practice and not just obsess about the outcome is most important.

Not understanding the steps to building confidence can pressure children into believing that they need to "be confident" even before the actions of practice. This can destroy their ability to choose "why not?" and in turn prevent them from unlocking their potential. Explaining to the child that he doesn't have to "be confident" but instead he will "become confident" can instill in him the power to say "why not." Armed with this knowledge, the child will be more inclined to embrace opportunities that unlock his full potential.

Exercise 2: What Is Confidence?

Start a conversation, grab a piece of paper, or download the *E-Journal for Children*.

Ask the child:

2.1 What does confidence mean to you?
   + Listen carefully to the responses.
   + Explain the meaning of confidence.
      Confidence is a feeling, but it is not a feeling with which you start out with. Confidence is a feeling that you develop after you practice.
   + Give an example of when you felt confident.

2.2 Think of a time when performing the actions of practice helped you become confident. How did it make you feel?

2.3 What is the difference between "be confident" and "become confident"?
   + Explain to the child that they do not have to be confident at something before they have performed the actions of practice. They will become confident after the actions of practice.

Factors That Affect Confidence

Confidence is moldable. It can be taught, it can be nurtured, and it can be grown. Like a muscle, confidence can grow.

Here are some factors that might contribute to a child's confidence:

1. **Misconceptions about confidence:** Not understanding confidence and the process of gaining confidence can be the biggest barrier. A child is surrounded by people who have their own spin on what confidence is. This can puzzle and overwhelm a child. The media and influencers' views on what embodies confidence can further confuse the child.

2. **Parenting styles:** How well-meaning adults view confidence can be passed down through generations. This needs to be examined to ensure children are receiving information about confidence that will be most helpful to them in their current context.

3. **Friends:** The perceptions of their friends have a great impact on the confidence of a child. In the company of other children who embody the 3C's of ACM, the child will be inclined to do so as well. On the other hand, being surrounded by bullies or any form of harassment can have a negative impact on the child.

4. **Mental or physical health concerns**: Any of these can affect a child's confidence. If you feel this is the case with a child you know, please seek the help of a licensed professional.

Do any of these factors apply to you and your previous discussions about confidence with a child? Having this awareness can help guide future discussions.

Creating a Circle of Confidence for the Child

As you've learned, a Circle of Confidence is a group of people the child sees as being positive and supportive. This group of supportive and well-meaning adults and children (who can also be both Rocks and Champions) might include parents, relatives, teachers, after-school providers, coaches and peers.

One of the most crucial elements of children developing confidence is to surround them with support. Rather than leaving children to wonder who's in their corner when they need support, we can help them identify the people who already have their back before they need to rely on them.

Exercise 3: Creating a Circle of Confidence and Community of Confidence

Start a conversation, grab a piece of paper, or download the *E-Journal for Children*.

Ask the child:

3.1   Who are the people in your life that you see as being positive and supportive of you?

    ✦   Have them make a list.

    ✦   Explain to the child that this list makes their Circle of Confidence.

        A Circle of Confidence is a group of people who the child sees as being positive and supportive of them.

3.2   Who out of these people are involved in your life on a day-to-day basis and take responsibility for you?

    ✦   Explain to them that these people are the Rocks in their life.

        A Rock is a person who is involved in your life and takes care of you. For example, a Rock is the person who might take care of you when you are sick.

3.3   Who are the people that you respect and trust and that you ask for feedback and advice?

+   Explain to the child that these are Champions in their life.

A Champion is a person who you ask for advice. For example, your science teacher maybe your Champion as you prepare for the upcoming science fair at school.

+   Explain to the child that there may be an overlap in Rocks and Champions.

3.4   Think about life situations in which you might reach out to someone and ask that person to be a part of your Circle of Confidence. Have them share with you.

For example, you want your grandmother to be a Rock but she lives in a different state. Perhaps you can call her and ask her if she would be willing to chat with you on a regular basis. If you want your neighbor to help you with your basketball skills, perhaps you seek permission from an adult in the household to reach out to them. Then you might ask your neighbor if they can play with you a couple times a week and show you how to improve.

+   Remind the child to seek agreement from people to be part of their Circle of Confidence, even if they haven't yet designated them as a Rock or Champion.

+   Remind them that staying connected to Rocks and Champions is important. Ask them to think about how often they will keep in touch with each person within their Circle of Confidence.

+   Help the child role-play these conversations. For example, if the child is trying out for the volleyball team and Aunt Susie is an athlete, reverse role-play with them. "Hello, Aunt Susie, how are you? I am excited to share with you that I want to try out for the volleyball team at school. I know you played sports in school. May I call you if I have any questions?"

Reverse role-plays are fun and effective. You can also help the child create an email outline or write a note to a potential member of their Circle of Confidence.

Dear Aunt Susie,

I hope you are doing well. I am excited to share with you that I am trying out for the volleyball team at school. I remember hearing stories about you being involved in sports as a kid. Can I reach out to you if I have any questions? If so, what would be the best way to connect with you?

Creating a Community of Confidence for Adults

Just as the child is encouraged to create a Circle of Confidence, a well-meaning adult should seek to develop a Community of Confidence, a support system that wants the adult to succeed in instilling confidence in a child. The well-meaning adult understands he or she isn't alone and can reach out to other Rocks and Champions in their Community of Confidence, to support the individual in instilling ACM in a child.

This group of supportive individuals once again can include both adults and children. As much as a teacher or coach might be part of your Community of Confidence, likewise a friend of the child might be a valuable member as well. Your Community of Confidence can help you and support you when you need advice. I know that I often rely on feedback from my daughter's teachers, coaches, and her friend Helena. At the risk of repeating myself, confidence is a team sport.

Grab a piece of paper for the following exercise.

- List individuals who are supportive of you and whose feedback you seek.
- How do you know them? What relationship do you currently have with these people?

- For what type of life situations would each of them be a good resource?

- From this list, which people will you connect with and ask if they agree to have this role in your life?

- How do you plan to deepen this relationship?

- Once you have earmarked who is in your community, make the effort to stay connected with these people.

- Reach out to them. You might say or write something as follows: "I see you as being supportive of me and the role that I play in (blank)'s life. Would it be okay for me to reach out to you for advice or feedback?"

Keep this list handy so you know how to access these resources. Keep these people apprised of your child's progress and growth.

Tending to these relationships and keeping them active will enhance the likelihood these people will step in and advise when needed.

The size of the Circle of Confidence or Community of Confidence does not matter. What is important is that there is one. Slowly over time it can be expanded.

Key Points:

- Discussions are more productive when a child is calm and not feeling highly emotional.

- The purpose of confidence education is to bring awareness to children that confidence building is a process.

- Not understanding the steps to building confidence can put pressure on children, that they need to be confident before the actions of practice.

- Confidence is malleable. It can be taught; it can be nurtured and grown.

CHAPTER 8

THE COURAGE TOOL KIT

Let us focus on each of the 3C's to see how each of them (individually and together) develop confidence in a child. True confidence comes from one part courage, one part character, and an abundant supply of commitment, but courage is still the crucial first step of instilling ACM in children.

The Need for Courage

In my line of work, I have noticed that many children, as well as well-meaning adults, confuse courage with confidence. Courage should not be confused with confidence. Courage is not confidence. It is the starting point, the beginning of the journey towards confidence building. To embark upon this journey, you *need* to have courage.

When Karishma and Rohan were in high school, I was at a point in my life when I didn't feel I had courage. My second marriage had begun crumbling. Karishma was a junior and Rohan was a freshman in high school. Maahi was barely two, but even as a toddler she could sense her parents were not getting along.

I raised my two older children as a single mother for most of their lives. Going through a divorce for a second time made me lose belief in myself. It was a difficult period in my life. I was a well-meaning adult with three children I was responsible for, but at that moment of time I lacked courage.

Courage is being afraid, knowing that there is risk involved and yet making the decision to do something anyway. Courage is feeling fear yet choosing to act. However, all I felt was defeat and questioned my actions. At that time, I lacked self-belief and was fearful of being a single parent to three children.

Left with no choice, I decided to rely on my Community of Confidence, which was my immediate family (all of whom lived in India). Karishma had moved to college and Maahi was two years old. Rohan was in high school. He needed my physical and emotional presence and I was unable to be there for him. I was in the "why me" phase of my life. At the same time, I was caring for a toddler.

My mother and my brother Manish visited me from India that summer. They saw my situation and offered to take Rohan to India for the remainder of high school. It was one of the most difficult decisions I have ever had to make. Sending my teenaged son to live in a country he had only visited a few times in his life was heart-wrenching. I knew when he returned, he would be off to college and he might never live with me again. Yet, I reluctantly sent Rohan to live with my parents because I understood he would be in better hands during this difficult stage of my life.

I remember the day I spoke to Rohan about this, as vividly as if it was yesterday.

"Rohan, how do you feel in this moment?" I asked.

"Good," Rohan, replied.

With the one-word check-in he sensed a discussion coming his way."

"Rohan, I really have a lot on my plate and I'm thinking it might be good for you to move to India for high school."

Rohan was taken aback. "India?" he asked. "Why, Mom?"

"Things aren't going well at home, and I am trying to cope with the divorce and Maahi," I responded honestly.

"I think you'll benefit from having your uncle and Pops as male role models. Your grandmother and Swati (Manish's wife) will take care of you."

"I've never been to school in India, I'm not sure how I'll do." Rohan was concerned.

"I know it's a huge step. But, if you believe in yourself, you'll be happy and successful in any school anywhere in the world."

"But I won't know anyone there! This is high school; people have already made cliques in their freshman year and I'm going to go there as a sophomore. What if I don't make any new friends?"

I found myself encouraging Rohan the way Pops did for me when I was the new kid in town. "I know you're nervous: let us just breathe for a moment. Think about it. If you accept the challenge to meet one new person a day, I think you could really enjoy your time there. And, you know what, find some fun doing so."

He moved to India in his sophomore year and lived with my parents and spent time with my brother Manish and his family as well. Rohan did not know what to expect from his new school or surroundings. Things he had taken for granted in the United States, like running hot water, were more complicated at my parents' home. Rohan quickly learned that to have a hot shower he had to first switch on the hot water geyser, as they are called. This was just one of the many adjustments to daily life that Rohan had to make in India. Even though I had enrolled him in a school connected to the American Embassy, outside of school, his broken Hindi was a barrier.

Rohan returned home after his high school graduation as a happy and fulfilled young man. His time overseas instilled in him empathy and gratitude. It made him a well-rounded young man ready to embark on his journey to become a doctor.

I always thought moving to India was a huge act of courage on Rohan's part. I'll never forget one of the first things Rohan told me when he returned.

"Mom, I know it was hard for you to send me away. How did you find the courage to do it?"

I was stunned. Though I didn't believe I was being courageous, Rohan viewed relying on my "Community of Confidence" as an act of courage. What I learned from that exchange is that asking for help is an act of courage in itself.

Well-meaning adults are often too hard on themselves. Some believe that if they do not embody a certain trait or value, they cannot help develop it in a child. That is far from the truth. It is acceptable to lean on others to get the help needed.

A child *needs* courage to get started. You may ask, "but how?" How do children learn to believe in themselves? How are they going to be equipped to face their fears? Instilling courage is a step-by-step process and I've put together a few tools you can use to help instill courage in the child.

INSTILLING COURAGE

Step 1: Believe in Yourself: The child believes she is equipped to perform the actions of practice.

Step 2: Face Fears: The child understands she doesn't need to be fearless; she needs to face her fears.

Step 1: Tools to Believe in Yourself

Believing in yourself means having faith in your own abilities. It means having the awareness and knowledge that your abilities are valuable. You know you have to still learn new skills but you believe in yourself at every stage of life. To help a child believe in himself, it is important to have the child first identify his strengths and areas for growth. The child must also be equipped to engage in positive self-talk and give affirmation to himself when facing a difficult situation.

Confidence isn't just about having strengths. A child who is aware of his areas that need growth and still has the courage to find opportunities in challenges is just as, if not more, powerful than a child who believes that he doesn't need to grow. That's why mindful evaluation also includes identifying such areas.

It is hard for most children to know exactly what their areas of growth are. In times when they are aware they may feel vulnerable. They worry about whether they will be ridiculed or laughed at. Remind the child that you are the Rock and/or Champion in his life and you are present to help him. Also share with him that everyone has areas of growth they are working on, not just him.

Exercise 4: Evaluating Strengths and Identifying Areas for Growth

Start a conversation, grab a piece of paper, or download the *E-Journal for Children*.

Ask the child:

4.1 What do you enjoy doing that you are proud of?

4.2 What qualities have helped you accomplish your goals?

4.3 Share something challenging you have overcome.

- Once he has answers, help the child consolidate the strengths into a list. This list can come in handy any time he needs a boost.
- Have the child conduct a mindful self-evaluation for areas of growth using the following questions

4.4 What are some of your areas for growth?

4.5 What is something that is challenging for you?

4.8 What makes it challenging?

- ✦ Once she has discussed or written down the answers, help the child identify common patterns in the answers. For example, a child might say, "I don't keep my stuff organized or I don't turn in my assignments on time."

- ✦ When having these conversations adults should be prepared to have to drill down into children's responses and ask more follow-up questions to really help them get to their strengths and areas for growth.

Step 2: Tools to Face Fears

Having fears is *not* the opposite of being confident. It is part of the journey to "become confident." To "become confident" means knowing that being afraid is okay provided coping mechanisms are in place to rely on. In my confidence education work and with my own children, I've observed that most children are very aware of their fears.

Children often believe that being afraid and being nervous are the same feelings, but they are not. Being afraid is being in a situation that is dangerous and can cause pain. For example, being stuck in an elevator or seeing a dangerous animal can cause a child to be afraid. Feeling nervous is being anxious or worried; it is more often a response to not knowing what will happen in a future situation, and thinking about the possibilities of negative outcomes or dangers that may or may not be present.

For example, nervousness is the feeling you have right before a big game, a test, or performance.

Feeling fearful or nervous is sometimes normal, and these feelings can be helpful in keeping us alert and safe. However, nervousness can also cause problems when it keeps us from taking action to accomplish our goals. The first step is to help the child identify the origin of fear.

Exercise 5: Identifying the Origin of Fear

Start a conversation, grab a piece of paper, or download the *E-Journal for Children*.

Ask the child:

5.1 What do you fear? Give examples of things of which you are afraid.

5.2 How do you feel when you are afraid?

5.3 How do you feel when you are nervous?

5.4 Look at the list of things you're afraid of and circle those you fear and those that make you nervous.

5.5 What do you do now when you are in situations that make you afraid or nervous?

   ✦ Inform the child that identifying the origin of fear and reflecting about one's fears is the first step towards determining which strategies might be helpful and when to use them.

Children need a reliable method to deal with these feelings. Rather than seeing fear as a barrier, they can use it as an opportunity to act—which is the foundation for developing confidence.

Having effective coping mechanisms is important in helping children face fear. They don't have to completely overcome their fears, but they should learn to face them.

The strategies in the following section are simple tools that can help children cope with occasional feelings of nervousness that arise when they are faced with new or challenging situations. These recommended coping strategies are drawn from experience, and from research on how best to reduce feelings of anxiety in children and teens. However, they are not a substitute for receiving therapeutic services.

NOTE: *If anxiety is holding children back from doing what they want to do even after trying out these tools, they may benefit from getting some additional support from a mental health professional.*

Research in the field of psychology shows that cognitive behavioral therapy techniques are effective in reducing symptoms of anxiety in children and teens.[4,5] Cognitive behavioral therapy involves learning about emotions and changing unhelpful patterns of thinking and behavior to improve functioning, and this book (or the ConfidentLee® program) includes some techniques that follow these same principles.

Coping Mechanisms

Positive Affirmations. Positive affirmations are simple, short, and powerful statements. They help a child be positive-minded and can stop self-sabotage. Well-meaning adults give affirmations through their encouragement, love, and support.

However, it is equally important for a child to create affirmations both for and by themselves. They can be a tool for the child to use throughout life.

Affirmations solidify the positive character traits the children use as a compass to guide their actions of practice. They are not just reciting a positive phrase; they are also priming themselves to be positive and resilient. Psychological studies have found these to be useful.[3]

Giving positive affirmations and having children create these for themselves may help combat negative or unhelpful thought patterns by shifting a child's focus to their strengths.

Self-affirmations that involve reflecting about a personal value such as kindness, gratitude, or contributions to others are also helpful and these values are discussed further in the next chapter. Psychological studies have found positive values-based affirmations to be useful in buffering the effects of stress.[3]

While affirmations are thoughts, and words, they do set the stage for positive actions. For example, in Part II, we discussed "character" and how it's all about being good to yourself and being good to others. Giving yourself a positive affirmation is also being good to yourself.

Positive affirmations motivate children and encourage positive change. They are ammunition against negative self-talk and train the brain to think in a positive and beneficial way. When children say, "I am confident," they are setting themselves to believe in their abilities. When they are taught to understand the steps to "become confident," they elevate this affirmation into reality.

Breathing and Shifting Focus. Breathing exercises also can help some individuals. It has helped me and the children we work with. Shifting focus is also an effective way for children to face fears. Facing fears sometimes requires pushing past fears by shifting focus away from the fear itself.

Relaxation techniques, like slow deep breathing and focusing attention on sensory experiences in the moment, are commonly incorporated in cognitive behavioral therapy and mindfulness interventions[1,5,6,7] to help with reducing stress and anxiety in children and adolescents.

A coping mechanism that I have often used, in the classroom and at home, encourages children to remain mindful of the moment they're in and not wonder about the outcomes. The actions of practice should always be more important than achieving any specific outcome. Shifting focus is also an effective way for children to face fears.

Non-avoidance. Exposure is another evidence-based technique for reducing anxiety[5] and it involves repeatedly engaging with a feared thing (e.g., a particular activity or situation) and tolerating the feelings that come with it until they decrease in intensity.[2] Put simply, exposure means gradually doing more and more of the thing that is feared and doing it consistently over time. It is much like committing to practice. At ConfidentLee®, we emphasize that children can and should use fear as an opportunity to take action rather than a reason to avoid doing what will help them to reach their goals. Facing fears doesn't mean that these feelings immediately disappear: it means tolerating the feelings and doing things any way will help to reduce them over time.

Sources:
1. Bluth, K., Gaylord, S.A., Campo, R.A., Mullarkey, M.C., & Hobbs, L. (2016). Making friends with yourself: A mixed methods pilot study of a mindful self-compassion program for adolescents. *Mindfulness, 7*, 479-492. https://doi.org/10.1007/s12671-015-0476-6

2. Craske, M. G., Treanor, M., Conway, C. C., Zbozinek, T., & Vervliet, B. (2014). Maximizing exposure therapy: An inhibitory learning approach. *Behaviour Research and Therapy, 58*, 10-23. https://doi.org/10.1016/j.brat.2014.04.006

3. Creswell, J. D., Dutcher, J. M., Klein, W. M., Harris, P. R., & Levine, J. M. (2013). Self-affirmation improves problem-solving under stress. *PloS one, 8*, e62593. https://doi.org/10.1371/journal.pone.0062593

4. Freidl, E. K., Stroeh, O. M., Elkins, R. M., Steinberg, E., Albano, A. M., & Rynn, M. (2017). Assessment and treatment of anxiety among children and adolescents. *Focus, 15*, 144-156. https://doi.org/10.1176/appi.focus.20160047

5. Higa-McMillan, C. K., Francis, S. E., Rith-Najarian, L., & Chorpita, B. F. (2016). Evidence base update: 50 years of research on treatment for child and adolescent anxiety. *Journal of Clinical Child & Adolescent Psychology, 45*, 91-113. https://doi.org/10.1080/15374416.2015.1046177

6. Jerath, R., Crawford, M. W., Barnes, V. A., & Harden, K. (2015). Self-regulation of breathing as a primary treatment for anxiety. *Applied Psychophysiology and Biofeedback, 40*, 107-115. https://doi.org/10.1007/s10484-015-9279-8

7. von der Embse, N., Barterian, J., & Segool, N. (2013). Test anxiety interventions for children and adolescents: A systematic review of treatment studies from 2000-2010. *Psychology in the Schools, 50*, 57-71. https://doi.org/10.1002/pits.21660

Exercise 6: Coping Mechanisms

Start a conversation, grab a piece of paper, or download the *E-Journal for Children*.

Ask the child:

6.1 Look at your strengths and craft positive statements about you.

- ✦ Explain to the child the concept of an affirmation. It is a phrase of emotional support or encouragement.
- ✦ If the child has written her affirmations, ask her to read them aloud.

NOTE: *In the E-Journal for Children, there are examples of affirmations to use. I've also included them in the Appendix under "Examples of Self-Affirmations."*

6.2 Think of something that brings a feeling of fear or nervousness. When faced with such feelings, it helps being present and mindful of the moment. Focus on your surroundings.

- ✦ Shift your focus from feeling fear to identifying five things you can see, four things you can touch, three things you can hear, two things you can smell, and one thing you can taste.
- ✦ Certain breathing exercises can help children cope with fear. For example, have the children pretend they have a flower in one hand and a candle in the other. Have them smell, the flower by taking a deep breath through their nose to fill the lungs with air. Then, have the children exhale and blow out the candle in the other hand.

Key Points

- Having fears is not the opposite of being confident.

- It is important to teach children how to face fears and for them to understand that some fears will be overcome and some not. What is important is to be able to face fears.

- To help children believe in themselves, it's important they first identify roadblocks and are open about what's getting in the way of performing their practice.

- Confidence isn't just about having strengths. Children who are aware of their areas for growth and use courage to find opportunities in challenges are powerful.

- As much as children can benefit from external feedback, they can also benefit from self-affirmations.

- Children should learn to identify whether they are afraid or nervous.

- Personal affirmations, mindfulness, and breathing are coping mechanisms.

CHAPTER 9

THE CHARACTER TOOL KIT

In the previous chapter, we took a deep dive into Courage. Courage gives children the freedom to explore and experiment in life. With courage, they begin to explore life's possibilities. Courage will get you in the door, but character will keep you in the room. That is why Character is the second step of instilling ACM in children. In this chapter, I will share strategies on how to develop positive character traits in a child.

The Purpose of Character

Teaching a child to possess positive character values is one of the most important skills they can learn. Positive character traits are when you simply recognize what is the right thing to do. They include traits such as kindness, gratitude, and being responsible. Well-meaning adults want children to be good to others and to themselves. Simply telling them to do so isn't enough. Setting a process to do so is needed.

> ## THE SECOND C: CHARACTER
>
> **Step 3: Be Good to Myself:** The child has positive values toward himself that guide actions.
>
> **Step 4: Be Good to Others:** The child has positive values that guides his actions toward others.

Embodying positive values is a step-by-step process. A well-meaning adult can give a child a structure to do so.

Positive character traits are instilled by both Rocks and Champions. Sister Karen was one of those Champions in Karishma's life. She was instrumental in introducing the purpose of character to Karishma and through her to me. When Karishma was in 10th grade, she told me her goal was to become the valedictorian of her high school. I reminded Karishma to work hard and get good grades; this was my job as her Rock. I wanted her to be well-rounded and academically strong.

One day, Karishma came home from school and shared with me a conversation she had with Sister Karen.

"Mom, I told Sister Karen I was working hard to become the valedictorian. I thought she'd say something about working hard or it's not easy—just like you tell me all the time."

"And?" I asked.

"And she told me that her personal view of a valedictorian is someone who has a positive attitude, is willing to learn, helps and encourages others, and wants to make a difference."

We were both a little baffled by it. Then, it sunk in: for Sister Karen good grades alone didn't cut it.

This conversation happened in 2008. At that point, I was a Rock in Karishma's life and Sister Karen was her Champion. Under Sister Karen's mentoring, Karishma took on many leadership roles at school. Her volunteering activities became personal to her and not just something to cross off a graduation checklist.

However, she began falling behind in her grades.

I sat her down one day.

"Your grades are slipping, Karishma, what's going on?"

"Mom, I'm trying," Karishma adamantly responded. "I'm involved in school projects and trying to do stuff that can impact others. It's like there just isn't enough time in the day."

I could see she felt pulled in different directions.

"Karishma, I know you want to do good for others. But it's important to be good to yourself too. You need to have better time management and take responsibility for your grades. Use a planner and track what you are spending your time on."

It wasn't just Karishma. I have had these "be good to yourself" discussions with Rohan and Maahi, as well as the children with whom I work.

Karishma began to prioritize both her academics and extracurricular activities. Tracking how much time she was spending on activities helped her find time to get her schoolwork done. Her grades improved.

Positive character values are beliefs you learn and embody all your life. Because Karishma was committed to them, she continued to soar in college and law school with her academics and volunteering. Sister Karen left a lifelong impact on Karishma. After graduating from law school, Karishma continues to be active in her alma mater's school board.

I always share with students how developing positive character values has no end point.

Building character is a lifelong process, and it starts with the child engaging in actions of practice that embody positive values each day. When the child is intentional about what he needs, this increases the probability of doing it. Character serves as a guide to the choices that children will make and can become a predictor of outcomes in school and in life.

A well-meaning adult may have his own list that is specific to his personal and family values. In the next few pages, I'm going to share with you some common positive values that can have a constructive impact on the life of a child.

Tools To Be Good to Yourself

All well-meaning adults want children to be happy. Instilling in a child character values that allow them to be good to themselves, from a young age, can help them grow up to become a happier adult.

Gratitude. Well-meaning adults play an important role in encouraging children to have an attitude of gratitude. Gratitude leads to optimism. Families that use kind words and express what they are thankful for develop deeper familial bonds. A simple thank you to a family member, friend, teacher, or instructor not only makes the other person feel good but also wins respect for the child. It all circles back to building one's own confidence.

Exercise 7: Having Gratitude

Start a conversation, grab a piece of paper, or download the *E-Journal for Children*.

Ask the child:

7.1 What are you thankful for?

7.2 Why are you thankful?

7.3 How can you give thanks?

-    ♦   Ask yourself the same questions.
-    ♦   Offer to do a gratitude share together.

NOTE: See Appendix for "10 Tips to Encourage Gratitude"

Sources:
1. Gabana, N. T., Steinfeldt, J., Wong, Y. J., Chung, Y. B., & Svetina, D. (2019). Attitude of gratitude: Exploring the implementation of a gratitude intervention with college athletes. *Journal of Applied Sport Psychology*, 31, 273-284. https://doi.org/10.1080/10413200.2018.1498956

2. Froh, J. J., Bono, G., Fan, J., Emmons, R. A., Henderson, K., Harris, C & Wood, A. M. (2014). Nice thinking! An educational intervention that teaches children to think gratefully. *School Psychology Review*, 43, 132-152. https://doi.org/10.1080/02796015.2014.12087440

3. Froh, J. J., Kashdan, T. B., Ozimkowski, K. M., & Miller, N. (2009). Who benefits the most from a gratitude intervention in children and adolescents? Examining positive affect as a moderator. *The Journal of Positive Psychology, 4*, 408-422. https://doi.org/10.1080/17439760902992464

Responsibility. Responsibility means being answerable for oneself and others. Learning to be responsible for oneself is a big step for a child. Whether it is keeping a room tidy or turning in assignments on time, responsibility affects confidence. When children are responsible, they gain the respect of those around them. This respect boosts their own image of themselves. It also makes them more likely to give themselves positive affirmations when challenged.

Exercise 8: Being Responsible

Start a conversation, grab a piece of paper, or download the *E-Journal for Children*.

Ask the child:

8.1   What does responsibility mean to you?

8.2   Why does responsibility matter?

8.3   What are you currently responsible for?

8.4   What can get in the way?

8.5   What is time management?

8.6   What can you do to manage your time better?

8.7   Which Rock or Champion in your Circle of Confidence can help you with responsibility and time management?

NOTE: See Appendix for "10 Tips to Encourage Responsibility" and "10 Tips to Encourage Time Management."

Time management. Time management is one of the biggest challenges children face. Some face this because they do not focus on it, or have not been taught how to manage their time or have overly busy schedules. Often with best intentions, distractions can also be a hindrance. Using a notebook or a calendar to earmark and set aside time for must-do and want-to-do activities can serve as a tool to help them track practice and stay on task.

Finally, the child needs free time. Free time is the best time for exploration and experimentation. Unstructured time gives the well-meaning adult a glimpse into where the child's mind goes when it isn't orchestrated.

Time management affects confidence because it gives the child the time for actions of practice.

Find Fun. Finding fun in practice is the biggest motivator to continue to practice. It means approaching life enthusiastically, as an adventure, not an ordeal. Finding fun means taking what one does and enjoying it. Anything can have an element of fun with the right mindset. For example, if a child wants to find fun in reading, she may decide to read aloud and be dramatic or perhaps orchestrate a performance in front of an imaginary crowd. Finding fun in practice is the key component for motivation to stay on task.

Exercise 9: Finding Fun
Start a conversation, grab a piece of paper, or download the *E-Journal for Children*.

Ask the child:
9.1   What is finding fun?
9.2   How can you find fun in what you practice?
9.3   What is a skill that you are practicing currently?
9.4   How could you find fun in this practice?

Note: See Appendix for "10 Tips for Finding Fun."

Tools To Be Good to Others

"Be good" is something adults often say to a child. To be good to and with others is about having kindness, accountability, positive social behaviors, and striving to make a difference in the world.

Kindness. Teaching kids to be kind to others is something that will stay with them throughout their lives. Children are hard-wired to be kind and helpful. When the well-meaning adult sets the expectation of kindness as a way of life, children begin to incorporate acts of kindness into their day-to-day life. To be kind, one needs empathy, which is the ability to understand and share the feelings of another.

Kindness comes from actions and words. It could be a child helping a neighbor rake leaves or it could be words of encouragement to a friend who is overwhelmed by a school project. It could also be something as simple as helping the checkout clerk at the grocery store bag groceries or thanking the wait staff at a restaurant for serving the meal. Regardless of the specific words or actions, acts of kindness not only make others happy, but make a child feel happier and more fulfilled.

Kindness boosts a child's confidence. When a child reflects upon his act of kindness or receives thanks for his actions, it strengthens his belief in himself.

Exercise 10: Being Kind to Others

Start a conversation, grab a piece of paper, or download the *E-Journal for Children.*

Ask the child:

10.1 What does kindness mean to you?

10.2 Why does it matter?

10.3 What acts of kindness can you perform?

Note: See Appendix for "10 Tips to Encourage Acts of Kindness."

Family Contributions. Responsibility is not just towards yourself, but also towards those around you. It starts at home. Behaving as a responsible member of the family encourages a child to pursue endeavors of greater impact. Helping with housework allows a child to view himself as an important contributor to the family and it strengthens family connections. If a child is responsible for loading and unloading a dishwasher, he is less likely to leave dishes on the kitchen table at home or on the lunch table at school. These small acts of responsibility build a child's confidence.

In addition, helping with household responsibilities equips children with life skills that they need to function in the real world. I urge well-meaning adults to call these responsibilities contributions and not chores. Children need to contribute to their family unit, no matter how young they are. Also encourage children to find ways to contribute at school and in their community.

Exercise 11: Acts of Contribution at Home

Start a conversation, grab a piece of paper, or download the *E-Journal for Children.*

Ask the child:

11.1 What can you do to contribute to your family?

11.2 How would that make your family feel?

11.3 How does that make you feel?

11.4 How can practicing responsibility at home develop confidence?

NOTE: See Appendix for "10 Tips for Family Contributions."

Social Behaviors. Being respectful and polite are commonly respected social behaviors. Greeting others warmly, showing positive body language, and using kind words such as "please" and "thank you" reveal a great deal about a child's character values. Children with these wholesome values will be well received and welcomed in all spheres of life. This acceptance will bolster the belief that the children have in themselves, and it develops their confidence.

Exercise 12: Social Behaviors

Start a conversation, grab a piece of paper, or download the *E-Journal for Children*.

Ask the child:

12.1 What do social behaviors mean to you?
12.2 In your opinion, what are some common positive social behaviors?
12.3 How can your positive social behaviors make others feel around you?

NOTE: See Appendix for "10 Tips for Positive Social Behaviors."

Make a Difference in the World. Children may be small, but they can make a big difference in the world. Whether it is by sending a care package to faraway members of the military or taking care of a local park, the act of helping others beyond family and friends can instill a sense of purpose.

Encouraging stewardship during childhood teaches the importance of contributing to society and the planet. Small acts can instill a child's desire to become a responsible world citizen. It's never too early to get started.

Karishma's favorite elementary school activity was being a member of the safety patrol. Today, as an attorney currently serving as a prosecutor, Karishma feels that being on safety patrol was her first taste of being responsible enough to make a difference in the world for others.

Exercise 13: Practicing Making a Difference in the World

Start a conversation, grab a piece of paper, or download the *E-Journal for Children*.

Ask the child:

13.1 What does make a difference in the world mean to you?

13.2 What can you do to make a difference in the world around you?
13.3 Why does making a difference matter?

NOTE: See Appendix for "10 Tips on Making a Difference."

Character gives courage direction. However, both Courage and Character lose luster without commitment. That's why having Commitment is a game changer. Confidence building is a process, and this process takes commitment to practice.

Key Points

- Teaching a child to develop and embody positive character values is one of the most important skills a child can learn. Positive character values are simply knowing and executing the right things to do.

- Positive character values are both toward oneself and others.

- Setting achievable actions, for positive character values we want to see in our children, can help them learn how to make good choices in life.

- Confidence is the outcome after actions of practice; thus, being responsible and managing time plays an important role in developing confidence in a child.

- When children are responsible, they gain respect of those around them.

CHAPTER 10

THE COMMITMENT TOOL KIT

I have discussed in detail the importance of courage and character. Like other positive character values such as kindness and gratitude, commitment isn't a trait with which children are born. They must develop these important attributes. Helpful and concerned adults again play a major role in developing the ability of having commitment.

The Power of Commitment

As parents and well-meaning adults, we know it is often possible to inspire a child to have courage. I am inclined to believe that most children are guided by positive values. The roadblock most often comes from a lack of commitment, follow-through, or practice. Regardless of the words you choose—be it hard work, follow-through or commitment—you are probably shaking your head in unison. You are probably saying, "Yes, that's right, Namita! All this talk about confidence being the outcome of actions of practice is well and good. But how do I get my child to have commitment?"

I know. I get it. Commitment to practice is difficult for most kids. I say this, not only as a confidence educator, but as a mother as well. Throughout the book I have repeatedly said that confidence is not a feeling with which you start, but rather it is the outcome of actions of practice.

THE THIRD C: COMMITMENT

Step 5: Regular Practice: The child commits to the practice, as needed.

Step 6: Better Practice: The child commits to elevating her practice through self-reflection and getting feedback.

Five years ago, my youngest daughter Maahi was enrolled in ballet. Every Wednesday at 5 p.m., I would drop her off at the ballet studio. She had asked to take these classes, and I was more than happy to encourage her to pursue her interest. The first recital was delightful. I thought she had the ambition and the potential to be a ballerina.

A few months later, I picked up Maahi from class. She looked despondent. In the car, I asked her, "What's up? Why the glum face?"

I could tell that she didn't want to talk. Maahi turned to look out the window at the snowfall. We were about to pull into the driveway when she burst out, "I don't want to learn ballet anymore."

I hadn't even come to a stop, and yet I jerked back.

"What do you mean?" I was puzzled and upset.

"I just don't want to do ballet," Maahi repeated.

My first response was to bribe her.

"If you continue to do ballet, then I will give you extra time to make slime on the weekends." Making slime is something Maahi loves to do. Unfortunately, bribery didn't work.

"Mom, I don't want to do ballet anymore. Sorry, I just don't." Maahi's mind was made up.

I tried everything from anger, threatening her with losing privileges, to others forms of bribery, but nothing would change her mind. Finally, I gave up. Maahi quit ballet. The beautiful teal blue ballet costume we had already bought for the upcoming recital would end up hanging, unworn, in her closet.

It was only years later that Maahi would confide in me she had messed up on a big dance step; she was frustrated and convinced herself that she'd never be able to get it. She didn't know how to ask for help and feared she was disappointing her teacher and her classmates. So, she took the easiest way out and quit.

Maahi didn't tell me about this at the time. I didn't ask. I was too focused on how I'd convince her to continue ballet rather than trying to figure out why she didn't want to stay. She did not know that she could reach out to me, her Rock, or other well-meaning adults for input.

Even today, when Maahi looks at her friends who've stuck to ballet and are now in competitive dance, I see regret in her eyes because ballet was something she had aspired to learn while growing up. For all the power of commitment that I teach, talk, and tout, I could not help my own child commit to learning a skill set. This plagued me for years. Quietly, it did the same for Maahi. For several years after the ballet incident, Maahi continued to perform self-choreographed dance routines in the family room. She hadn't lost the interest, but possibly the courage for dance classes. I applauded her for these impromptu dance performances.

Finally, the day came when Maahi asked to enroll her in dance again.

I sat Maahi down and asked her why she wanted me to enroll her in another dance class. Maahi told me her goal was to learn to dance so she could perform at family and formal events. I told her if she was going to enroll in dance school, she must promise to stick to learning this form of dance until the final performance, even if she had second thoughts about pursuing this skill set. I also told her it was okay to ask for help if she felt unsure about any dance moves. We made an agreement that she could not drop out of this dance class no matter how difficult or how disinterested she was. She had to stick it out until a recital, final game, or performance.

The time span I chose for Maahi isn't backed up with research. It is a duration of time I felt was appropriate for Maahi to see the beginning and end of the tunnel.

Also, I asked her to create her Circle of Confidence and list the people, including well-meaning adults and peers, she could rely on for help. I asked her to reach out to them to confirm that they would be supportive, if needed.

I took it upon myself to create a Community of Confidence list. I reached out to Ms. Cindy, Maahi's dance teacher, on my own. I shared Maahi's struggles with her. She agreed to be part of my Community of Confidence. Maahi also wanted Ms. Cindy to be part of her Circle of Confidence, so I urged Maahi to make the "ask" herself.

Maahi enrolled in dance, and she started with great enthusiasm. Things went well for a few months and then Maahi once again began losing interest in dance. I must admit, even though dance is an after-school activity, I felt as if my world was crumbling.

Thoughts crept into my head: "Is my daughter lacking follow-through? Does she lack effort? Will she ever stick to a project or activity? Where have I fallen short as a mother?"

Just as every concerned parent does, I first blamed myself and tried to figure out where I was deficient in my parenting skills. "What is going on, Maahi?"

"I shouldn't have asked to take up dancing," Maahi said with regret. "I just don't feel confident I can ever be a dancer."

I recoiled at those words. Maahi had heard me say a thousand times, you don't have to feel confident to give something a shot; confidence is the outcome of practice. I am Maahi's Rock, but I knew she needed a Champion.

I asked for a meeting with Ms. Cindy. As a talented dancer and a no-nonsense teacher, Ms. Cindy held herself and her students to a high level of expectations. She expected them to practice. And Maahi was *not* practicing.

I figured out Maahi was not committed to her practice. Perhaps this happened in ballet? I had to park that thought. It's tough, but looking in the rear-view mirror doesn't help parenting either.

I felt shattered by this experience. If, after years of teaching the 3C's of Confidence, I had faltered with my own child, how could I be a confidence educator for other children? I sat Maahi down. Once again, I had no other choice but to rely on Pops' mantra: "Be brave. Be good. Work hard. Find fun. Be happy." I had Maahi break down each step of the mantra to help her stick to dancing until the recital.

Ballet had me realize that if it wasn't important to her, it wasn't worth banging heads over. Maahi agreed to stick to it until after the recital, Ms. Cindy reminded Maahi that the recital was five months away and asked her to make practice fifteen minutes a day and to record her daily practice. She also asked Maahi to commit to sending in video recordings of her practice.

Maahi knew her duration of commitment and decided it wasn't forever, so she might as well practice. She made a notebook to log the date and the length of time practiced and shared it with her teacher. Every time I caught her practicing, I applauded her positive values of organization, commitment, and follow-through. Maahi knew it was just a matter of a few weeks before she could be done with dance and with dance practice. That made it easier for her to commit to the actions of practice. Making an action plan to commit to practice helped her stay on track. Regular practice improved Maahi's dancing abilities and Ms. Cindy pointed that out to her.

Receiving praise for her effort reinforced Maahi's desire for practice. Every bit of improvement gave her a feeling of accomplishment. What anger and bribery could not accomplish for ballet, feedback from a member of Maahi's Circle of Confidence did, much to my relief. Soon Maahi began asking for feedback from her teacher and peers. With regular feedback, her dance practice became even better. When Maahi struggled with a particular step, she knew who to rely on. Better practice helped her improve her dancing skill even more. Her motivation now came from progress.

Maahi became more confident in her dancing artistry. The positive outcome of effort has given her confidence in her dancing abilities. I saw courage, character, and commitment lead to confidence. It is a circuitous answer, but each step is relevant.

I reminded Maahi she had become a confident dancer after actions of practice. "Maahi, you were brave, and stuck it out. You made an action plan. You worked hard on following through. You've become a confident dancer, and you seem happier."

Maahi has since committed to dance for years and plans to continue doing so. There are moments when she gets overwhelmed and says she needs to quit, but then realizes that the window to quit is not open. She then just carries on with her practice. This experience has made her more thoughtful about which skills she decides to pursue, knowing commitment to practice is crucial.

If Maahi decides to stop learning any skill set, I have to let her make that decision during the agreed upon window of time. We also have an understanding that I will not remind her to practice. It has to be important to her, and she has to be motivated to do so. Maahi knows that her reward is having an opportunity to learn the lifelong skill of dancing. Nothing more, nothing less.

Need to Learn vs. Want to Learn Skills

Dance is an activity that interests and challenges Maahi. I call it the "want to learn" skill in her life. She is now engaged to practice on her own. Although I would be remiss if I did not admit my approach is different with her academics—which, in my view, is a "need to learn" skill. In "need to learn" skills, Maahi has autonomy over where and when she practices. If she has math homework, she gets to decide where in the house and what time she chooses to complete the assignment. She does not, however, have the choice to not complete the homework. Finding fun in these need to learn skills is what keeps her going.

"Need to learn" skills are things that just need to get done. You may or may not agree with me, but parenting is subjective.

Exercise 14: Want to Learn and Need to Learn Skills

Start a conversation, grab a piece of paper, or download the *E-Journal for Children*.

Ask the child:

14.1 What are those skills that you believe you want to learn? Make a list of those.

14.2 Ask the child to call it the Want to Learn skills.

14.3 What are those skills that you believe that you need to learn? Make a list of those.

14.4 Ask the child to call this list the Need to Learn skills.

14.5 What are some similarities and differences between these two lists?

Tools for Regular Practice

With courage, a child has set the goal to learn a skill. By embodying positive character values, a child makes actions plans. Now it's time to execute the power of commitment and perform the actions of practice.

Each well-meaning adult might have a different "want to learn" and "need to learn" skills lists. The items on the list will differ from adult to adult, and from child to child. But the common denominator is that there is a list.

I believe the connotation of the word "practice" needs to change in the mind of a child. Whether a child needs to learn math or how to clean a room or a skill like a sport or music, he must recognize progress comes from practice. Instilling the attitude to practice instead of "trying" can change the child's approach to commitment. Instilling the practice attitude is a game changer.

As a reminder, practice is to perform an activity repeatedly with the intent to make progress. However, the term "practice" has earned a negative connotation. Before we tell a child to practice, we need to reprogram the meaning of the word "practice" for both the adult and the child. Practice doesn't have to be a stressful experience. It also doesn't have to take a long time. Short spurts of practice can make a big impact as well. Understanding this will encourage children to "practice" more often. When the word "practice" is used for fun endeavors such as family games, baking, and sports, it can change the meaning of the word "practice" in a child's mind. It evens the playing field for the word "practice" in need to learn and want to learn activities. It sounds simple but it is impactful because words *do* matter.

Keep in mind that character values are also things that need to be practiced. Applauding the child for practicing positive character values will help the child view the word "practice" as a positive action.

For example, when a child hears the word "practice" in contexts such as these-"You practiced being a good big sister today by watching your brother" or "Helping unload the dishwasher was you practicing contributing to your family" the-child sees the word "practice" in a positive light. Therefore, when the child hears phrases like "practice the piano" or "practice math problems" it reprograms the meaning of the word "practice" in their brains.

Exercise 15: Reprogramming the Meaning of the Word "Practice"

Start a conversation, grab a piece of paper, or download the *E-Journal for Children*.

Ask the child:

15.1 What actions do you practice regularly that you're proud of?

15.2 Offer to make a list of what the child practices that you think they should be proud of.

15.3 Make a list of positive actions the child engages in where the word "practice" can be used.

15.4 Let us share what is on each of our lists.

+ Use the word "practice" in these conversations. For example: "Good job practicing tidying up your toys!"

Once a positive connotation has been established for the word "practice", remind the child of the importance of committing to learning a skill for an agreed upon duration of time. This is extremely important in encouraging practice in a child's life. Even "need to learn" skills are manageable if the child knows there's an end point to it.

Setting a duration of time is not easy and this should be set up in concert with the child. Knowing that they were involved in the process will make them more likely to stick to it. Something that I use with Maahi is sticking to learning a skill for the duration of a semester or a school year. You and the child that you are working with will come up with something that works for your situation.

Often, to learn any skill, the process starts by making the skill a goal. A goal is something the children decide is important to them and they are willing to work hard to achieve. Goals for children can be difficult if they are not child sized. A child-sized goal is one that the child is involved in setting and the well-meaning adult ensures is an achievable goal.

To achieve that goal requires a child to have courage to set a goal, the character to make an action plan based on good values, and the commitment to follow through with actions of practice. For example, if children want to make the track team, they will make an action plan to practice running for fifteen minutes a day. The actions of practice are what ultimately builds their confidence. Starting small is crucial. Small wins build motivation to strive for bigger achievements.

Exercise 16: Goal Setting

Start a conversation, grab a piece of paper, or download the *E-Journal for Children*.

Ask the child:

16.1 What skills would you like to learn or improve?

16.2 Pick one of these skills to work on.

16.3 Break down the goal step by step.

16.4 Ask a member of your Circle of Confidence if this is an achievable goal.

16.5 To achieve this goal, what actions of practice will be needed?

16.6 Ask a Rock or Champion their suggestion on what actions of practice will be needed to achieve this goal.

16.7 How often will you perform the practice?

16.8 How long will each practice be?

16.9 How will you track your practice?

16.10 For what duration of time do you commit to practice?

Developing these skills of goal setting and making action plans early on is beneficial. Such behaviors will help open the possibilities for new experiences/skill sets.

Once the goal has been set, an action plan needs to be made by the child that outlines the actions of practice. This practice cannot be sporadic; it must be done repeatedly to make progress. Actions plans should also be written. A goal without a plan ends up becoming a dream. Having to record if the actions of practice are done has a positive effect on the commitment to perform practice.

During this process, asking questions that cannot be answered with a "yes" or "no" is critical. I wish I had done so with Maahi's ballet class. I wish I would have asked her more specific questions. Instead of asking her why she was quitting, I spent more time telling her not to quit.

Perhaps if I had asked Maahi specific questions, it might have steered her to share with me what challenge she was facing.

Exercise 17: Being Supportive of the Child

Start a conversation, grab a piece of paper, or download the *E-Journal for Children.*

Ask the child:

17.1   How can I support you to achieve your goal?

17.2   Who else can support you?

It is important, particularly for younger children, that they learn to find fun in learning. Anything can be fun, including need to learn skills. Math can be used at the toy store. English can be used to read directions at the park. Science can be used on a hike or nature walk. Fun helps foster the desire to practice.

Tools for "Better Practice"

Putting time into practice is only valuable if the quality of practice is improving. Children will face obstacles as they practice. To elevate their practice to better practice it is helpful to identify potential obstacles.

Some children might face difficulty with a particular aspect of the skill just as Maahi struggled with a particular dance step, or Karishma by having too much on her plate. Others might face distractions from electronics or friends.

The presence of a well-meaning adult can make all the difference in a child's life. The child can rely on the Circle of Confidence to overcome these obstacles. To do so, a child must learn to identify the origin of these obstacles. For most children, these obstacles are either distractions or challenges.

Obstacle. Children will face hindrance in the way of their progress. These hindrances are obstacles in the way of progress. Many obstacles can be differentiated between being distractions and challenges.

Distraction. Children face many distractions, such as too much social-ization, electronics, and social media. Often these distractions make it difficult for them to stay on task. A member of the Circle of Confidence can provide coping mechanisms that can help the child stay on track. Using a journal to jot down action plans and tracking progress of actions of practice is another effective way to garner awareness of distractions. Self-reflecting can shed light on patterns of what are common dis-tractions. With this awareness a child can reach out to their Circle of Confidence for feedback and suggestions.

Challenge. In the process of practice, the child can often hit a roadblock and face challenges. These could be lack of knowledge or tools. Finding role models for the child in their field of interest is another strategy. If the child is into sports, find an athlete. If she is into music, find a musician. If he loves to read, have him join a book club. Find champions that personify A Confident Mindset™.

For some children, having a discussion where they can look at the situation from the outside in and distancing themselves from the situation is helpful. For younger children, reading stories where the plot is about overcoming obstacles is another avenue to stage the discussion of confidence.

Exercise 18: Identify and Categorizing Obstacles

Start a conversation, grab a piece of paper, or download the *E-Journal for Children*.

Ask the child:

18.1 What is something you're working on that's important to you?

18.2 What can get in the way of achieving this goal?

- Explain to the child that this is an obstacle in the way of their achieving their goal.
- Explain what an obstacle is.
  An obstacle is what comes in the way of making progress.

18.3 What kind of obstacles might you face?
+ Explain obstacles might be challenges or distractions.

18.4 What is a challenge?
A challenge is something with which you need help, and you can rely on your Circle of Confidence for support.

18.5 What is a distraction?
A distraction is when your choices hold you back.
+ Explain that possessing positive character values of time management and responsibility can help you.

18.6 Is this obstacle a challenge or a distraction?
18.7 If it's a challenge, who in your Circle of Confidence can help you?
18.8 If you're distracted, what are the distractions?
18.9 Who or what can help you stay on track?

As children perform actions of practice, they need to assess for themselves how they are doing. Reflecting on their actions and behaviors to meet their goals can help children with self-awareness, self-regulation, and impulse control. They become mindful of their actions. Reflecting on what action worked and what didn't will allow them to make things work better next time.

Rocks and Champions can use the Glow and Grow practice to give feedback and suggestions. Giving advice to children can help them overcome obstacles.

A Glow is an authentic compliment because children know if it is or isn't. A Grow is an opportunity for the child to develop based on feedback. Both Rocks and Champions give Glows and Grows.

Exercise 19: Self-Reflection and Glow and Grow

Start a conversation, grab a piece of paper, or download the *E-Journal for Children*.

Ask the child:

19.1   Are you doing the actions of practice?

19.2   If yes, what can you do better?

19.3   If no, what's getting in the way?

19.4   Let me explain what a Glow and Grow is.

19.5   You always start with a one-word check-in.

19.6   Always ask for permission before giving feedback.

19.7   Start with a positive. Surely there is something that has been done well.

19.8   Follow by giving a suggestion.

19.9   Both the Glow and the Grow should be specific.

19.10   Finish with a one-word Check-in.

A few years ago, Maahi redecorated her bedroom. She picked the color scheme of silver and yellow. As we were putting up wall art, family photos, trophies, and certificates, Maahi asked if she could hang up the teal blue ballet costume. I was surprised.

"Teal does not go with your color scheme," I reminded Maahi. "And that isn't the decoration theme of your room. Why do you want to hang that dress on the wall?"

Unbothered, Maahi replied, "It reminds me that I quit dancing too soon, and I don't ever want do that again. Next time I want to quit, I'm going to look at my ballerina dress and it'll remind me not to give up."

My eyes welled up with tears. "Do you really want to do that?"

"The trophies remind me I can learn and grow at anything I want," Maahi further reflected. "This dress reminds me to not give up. It's not a failure, Mom. It is a reminder."

Maahi wanted to showcase her failure next to her accomplishments and was determined to do so. As parents we are inclined to showcase awards, medals, and certificates of accomplishment for our children. Maybe having a bird's-eye view of a failure, a lost opportunity, or chance not taken should have its place next to the winning memorabilia. Possibly some future successes will come from such reminders. Maahi had turned her failure into a mistake and, thus, it was inspiring and not devastating.

As the well-meaning adult in her life, the teal blue dress reminds me I need to work on being a better parent. Perhaps I need to ask deeper, more probing questions. Perhaps I need to have her create a Circle of Confidence that can support her. Maybe I need to focus more on the acts of practice and progress than the goal itself. The teal blue ballerina dress reminds me to not give up too quickly or too soon as a parent. Parenting for confidence surely takes time, patience, and the know-how of the process.

A Confident Mindset™ will give the child the power of why not to explore and experiment life. Failures are equally important as successes. It is important for children to find why they faced failure and view it as a mistake to learn from and not something to be ashamed of. Not learning to face failure leaves children vulnerable to being depressed and anxious. It also affects their desire to try new things and their ability to say "why not." There is a lot of pressure on children to be winners in whatever they do. The ability to find, evaluate, and understand the reason for the failure is crucial. A well-meaning adult can help a child understand both how to face a failure and view it it as an area for growth.

Exercise 20: Processing All Outcomes

Start a conversation, grab a piece of paper, or download the *E-Journal for Children*.

Ask the child:

20.1   Was there a time you didn't achieve a goal?

20.2   What struggles did you face?

20.3   What actions of practice could you have done differently?

20.4   Think of a time you were successful at something? What was it?

20.5   What actions of practice made you successful?

20.6   How could you improve these actions of practice?

20.7   Who in your Circle of Confidence could have supported you?

Children need to understand that not achieving goals is a part of life. They need to know such situations are a normal part of learning and that everyone experiences setbacks at some point. Feedback on how to better practice is often more important than the applause received upon reaching a goal.

Well-meaning adults sharing personal stories of similar experiences and how they dealt with it makes them relatable to a child. Sometimes the child might feel frustrated or confused. The intervention of a well-meaning adult can help the child get back on track.

Likewise, learning to face success is equally important. Focusing on achieving a goal is less important than appreciating the actions of practice that led to this achievement. This approach further ingrains in children that, regardless of whether they achieved a goal or not, it's the actions of practice that ultimately matter. These actions of practice develop unstoppable confidence in the child. When you help your children celebrate a success, whether it is winning the race, getting a high grade on an exam, or something else, you should certainly praise the accomplishment. However, your praise should never focus solely on the grade or the award. You should always emphasize the actions of practice—the efforts and dedication—rather than the end result.

Key Points

- Confidence is the outcome of actions of practice. To follow through with commitment, a child must prioritize regular practice and better practice.

- To achieve any goal requires actions of practice which in turn builds confidence.

- Putting time into practice is only valuable if the quality of practice is improving. The child will face obstacles. Therefore, having a Circle of Confidence can help the child get through the challenges.

- It's important for children to find out why they faced failure and view it as a mistake to learn from and not something to be ashamed of.

- There's a lot of pressure on children to be confident when they learn something new. Therefore, it is imperative that children be aware that confidence will come after actions of practice.

FINAL THOUGHTS

Thank you for taking the time to read *The Power of Why Not*. You are now ready to make a lifelong impact on a child's life. Regardless of whether you are a Rock and/or a Champion, you can now turn every child into a champ. I'm going to leave you with a few final thoughts.

The commitment to create this body of work meant write, rewrite, scrap, and write again. I am grateful for those who kept me going and showed me kindness in words and actions.

Many times, I was frustrated and felt like giving up. I would ask myself, why am I writing this book? The answer always came back, why not! If this book instills ACM in just one child, I believe my why not approach has made a difference.

I've shared with you my personal journey, yet writing this book is my biggest act of ACM. First, I am not an educator. I fell into this profession by accident. The why not approach turned this opportunity into a gift. Possessing ACM has empowered me to position myself as a self-proclaimed confidence educator and start the movement for confidence education.

Much of what I have shared with you might seem like common sense. However, often what is common sense is not common practice. Teaching children to become confident is possible and can be done by every adult, parent or not. It may not result in all children becoming *the* best, but it certainly can lead them to becoming their personal best. It will alleviate the boundaries children put on themselves because they feel no pressure to "be confident" and, instead, they will follow a step-by-step process to "become confident."

I set out to change the world for all children by writing *The Power of Why Not*. It took courage to face my past and share my vulnerabilities. However, when you set out to empower others, the first person you empower is yourself.

The principles of Pops' mantra ("Be brave. Be good. Work hard. Have fun. Be happy.") and ACM (Courage - Character - Commitment) are not just for kids; they apply to everyone. I want confidence building to become a tradition, not just in my home or yours, but in all homes around the world. Today you are impacting a child. Tomorrow this child will impact another. With each generation, my hope is we pass down the process of building confidence. That's how the confidence movement will spread.

Brigadier Shyam Prasad, my Pops, I salute you. Thank you for making me become confident and helping others become confident. It is because of you that my struggles became my strength. I know you never got to read this book. You left us on your final journey while I was still writing it. You'll be proud to know you've left your legacy of confidence in Manish and me, and also in my children, Karishma, Rohan, and Maahi. Now I get to share your mantra and the approach of A Confident Mindset™ to all children worldwide.

APPENDIX

Examples of Self-Affirmations

- I am courageous.
- I am unique.
- I can do hard things.
- I don't give up.
- I can make a difference.
- I am ready for new challenges.
- I make good choices.
- I believe in myself.
- I set goals.
- I am capable.
- I get better every day.
- I welcome feedback.
- I make progress.
- I am valuable.

10 Tips to Encourage Gratitude

1. Be thankful for a special person in your life.
2. Be thankful for something someone has done for you.
3. Be thankful for an object you have.
4. Take the time to reflect on the best part of each day.
5. Take the time to write a thank you note to someone.
6. Find the good in something that didn't turn out as you wanted.
7. Think about someone who made you laugh.
8. Think about someone who helped you.
9. Be thankful for something that brought you joy.
10. Be thankful for a special time with someone.

10 Tips to Encourage Being Responsible

1. Use an alarm to wake up for school.
2. Make their bed every morning.
3. Set out their clothes.
4. Keep their belongings organized.
5. Keep their bag pack organized.
6. Use a planner to record assignments.
7. Keep their space tidy.
8. Pick up after themselves.
9. Eat healthy.
10. Do some form of exercise.

10 Tips for Finding Fun

1. Turn it into a game.
2. Include some movement or dance.
3. Add music.
4. Find a friend to do it with.
5. Do it with a Rock or Champion.

6. Give what you are doing a silly name.
7. Add creativity like art or drama.
8. Race against time.
9. Reward yourself.
10. Use technology (with permission).

10 Tips to Encourage Acts of Kindness

1. Give a heartfelt compliment.
2. Give someone a hug.
3. Cheer up a friend who isn't feeling well.
4. Help someone with a chore.
5. Smile at someone.
6. Leave a friendly note for someone.
7. Make someone laugh.
8. Clean up a mess that you did not make.
9. Include someone in a game you are playing.
10. Let someone in front of you in a line.

10 Tips to Encourage Acts of Contribution at Home

1. Getting the mail.
2. Helping with dishes.
3. Helping setting and cleaning up after a meal.
4. Taking out the garbage.
5. Tidying up and organizing.
6. Helping with meal preparation.
7. Helping with laundry.
8. Helping with gardening.
9. Caring for a pet.
10. Helping with house cleaning.

10 Tips to Demonstrate Good Social Behavior

1. Making introductions. Many times, children meet new people and do not know how to introduce themselves or how to introduce friends to each other.
2. The proper way to sneeze or cough.
3. Greeting visitors and saying goodbye to them.
4. Knocking on doors before entering a room.
5. Asking for and not reaching for things.
6. Washing one's hands before meals.
7. Not interrupting others when talking. Saying "excuse me" if interruption is necessary.
8. Asking to be excused at the end of the meal instead of just getting up and leaving.
9. Holding the door open for others.
10. Writing thank you notes when they receive gifts.

10 Tips to Encourage Making a Difference in the World

1. Help a neighbor.
2. Help a teacher.
3. Help at an animal shelter.
4. Donate items.
5. Send cards to military members.
6. Make cards for people at nursing homes.
7. Help clean up a community area.
8. Collect items for a community food pantry.
9. Collect winter clothing for the homeless.
10. Volunteer at a homeless shelter.

10 Tip to Encourage Time Management

1.   Set a bedtime.
2.   Make a monthly calendar.
3.   Make a schedule for each day.
4.   Make a to-do list.
5.   Set priorities.
6.   Have assigned play time.
7.   Use a timer.
8.   Wear a watch.
9.   Have set mealtimes.
10. Have set study times.

GLOSSARY

3C's of A Confident Mindset™

COURAGE

The first C, which stands for the word "courage," is believing in yourself and your abilities. Having courage does not mean children are without fear; it means being able to face their fears.

CHARACTER

The second C, which stands for "character," refers to personal values. It's the inner compass that guides actions of practice, decisions, and judgments in life towards self and others. Embodying good values guides the action plans to achieve goals.

COMMITMENT

The third C, which stands for "commitment," is the effort to engage in practice. Regular practice leads to progress. Self-reflection and feedback help improve or better one's practice.

1. A Confident Mindset™ (ACM)

ACM describes a frame of mind that possesses courage, character, and commitment.

2. Actions of Practice

Doing an activity regularly according to an action plan.

3. Better Practice

Committing to elevating one's practice through self-reflection and getting feedback.

4. Champion

A Champion is a person you respect and trust. This individual will encourage you and give you feedback to help you better your practice.

5. Character

Character is having positive values that are recognized as the right thing to do for yourself and for others.

6. Circle of Confidence

A collective group of Rocks and Champions who are involved in supporting and encouraging children to become more confident and successful in life make up the Circle of Confidence for the child.

7. Commitment

Commitment is being dedicated to actions of practice.

8. Community of Confidence

A collective group of people who are a resource and provide feedback and encouragement to well-meaning adults in their journey to instill confidence in a child.

9. Confidence

Confidence is the outcome of the actions of practice, not a feeling you have before you practice.

10. Courage

Courage is possessing a can-do attitude. It's the quality that enables people to believe in themselves and face a difficult or fearful situation.

11. Mindset

A mindset is an individual's view, a unique lens, on the world. Mindset is the attitude with which we approach situations in life. It is a state of mind based on personal beliefs. These beliefs guide our actions in life.

12. Regular Practice

Committing to the practice, as needed.

13. Rock

A Rock is involved in a child's life on a day-to-day basis. The Rock takes responsibility for the child. This person provides feedback and encourages the child to practice.

14. Skill Set

A skill set is the set of skills that a person has developed to use in life. A skill set is the combination of knowledge and abilities that an individual has developed through life and work.

15. Well-Meaning Adults

Parents, educators, and other adults who have an influence over a child's life.

ABOUT THE AUTHOR

NAMITA is the founder of ConfidentLee®, an outcome-based confidence building process for creating A Confident Mindset™. This program is designed to encourage children to unlock and develop their full potential both at school and in life. She is an author, speaker and confidence educator who is passionate about helping children develop a "why not" approach.

Experiences at her learning centers made her realize that children, parents, teachers, coaches and after-school programs need to have a unified approach about what confidence is, why it matters and how to instill it. She has started a movement for confidence education. Namita believes confidence is a mindset and not a skill set. Before a child is taught any skill set, they must be taught how to become confident. Empowered with A Confident Mindset™, a child can learn any skill set.

She can be reached through her website at www.namitaprasad.com where she offers free downloads and resources. An accompanying journal for children is available on her website. You can also connect with her at https://www.facebook.com/confidenceeducator.

THE POWER OF WHY NOT

A GUIDE TO RAISING CONFIDENT CHILDREN WHO ARE HAPPY, KIND AND SUCCESSFUL

✦ ✦ ✦

To learn about A Confidence Mindset™ visit
https://namitaprasad.com
(Access easy to use resources)

Sign up for FREE confidence building resources
https://namitaprasad.com/freebies/#join

For confidence building programs for children visit
https://confidentlee.com/

Made in the USA
Las Vegas, NV
10 April 2022

47144447R00095